BETWEEN UKRAINE
AND RUSSIA

WORKING IN AMERICA

BETWEEN UKRAINE AND RUSSIA

WORKING IN AMERICA

SUSAN GOLD

FCP

Full Court Press
Englewood Cliffs, New Jersey

First Edition

Copyright © 2024 by Susan Gold

Published in the United States of America
by Full Court Press, 601 Palisade Avenue
Englewood Cliffs, NJ 07632
www.fullcourtpress.com

ISBN 978-1-953728-33-3
Library of Congress Control Number: 2024912939

Editing and Book Design by Barry Sheinkopf
Author Photograph by Barry Sheinkopf

To Dr. Robert Schumeister
and David R. Zimmerman

Everything that lives and endures
For more than a day after we die
Is eternal.
We live in the eternity of others.
We are their eternity.

—Yehuda Amichai, *"Posthumous Fragments"*

Acknowledgements

Editorial assistance and guidance for this book came from Barry Sheinkopf, Director of The Writing Center and Publisher of Full Court Press in Englewood Cliffs, New Jersey. I am grateful as well to my dear friend and colleague Alex Motyl for reading this memoir, for his editorial assistance, and for his perfect transliterations. David Zimmerman, my partner and a journalist, corrected my prose; with the gift of love we survive. Also important is my work with Dr. Robert Schumeister, who has encouraged the crystallization of my life in America into writing. Many thanks, finally, to Jasper Dionisio, whose computer skills and expertise with the English language helped me write this book.

Illustrations

1
BEGINNINGS

I was born in Złoczów, Poland, and lived in Włodzimierz Wołynski, the home of my father's family. Włodzimierz was first mentioned in chronicles of the tenth century as a fortified trading town, second only to Kiev in importance as a seat of the Eastern Church.

The first Jewish presence in the town goes back to the twelfth century. Following the Tatar Mongol raids at that time, the presumed descendants of the Khazars, a Turkish tribe, converted to Judaism in the eighteenth century. Włodzimierz was later annexed by Russia and served as a county seat (*gubernya*) for the province of Volhynia.

Grandpa Jacob told us that our family had entered the area in the late Middle Ages after being driven east by the Church, at which time the family settled in Włodzimierz, a county seat of the Eastern Church.

After Russian annexation, in the mid- and late-nineteenth century, the social structure of the higher orders changed. Russian family dynasties in the Russian Empire, founded on service to the tsars, became the new owners of the estates, quarries, and timber houses. Jewish businessmen were able to lease and manage this land. Further down the class structure came the German merchants and the Jewish tradesmen, artisans, tailors, carpenters, butchers, and bakers living close to the market, in its small ghetto.

The Gellers were among the few Jewish professionals living in the "suburbs" of Włodzimierz. The family lived in the only brick house in town. The house was actually a compound of three apartments: ours, my uncle's, and my grandparents', each with its own bedrooms, but they shared a common kitchen and dining room.

I have allowed myself to remember some happy and

magical early-childhood times in that country house, especially those on the round wooden veranda with the circular wooden table, rounded wooden chairs, and two rocking chairs, where I played, my imagination running wild, riding strong-willed, able-bodied, fast horses that stood many hands tall. I can still feel light, warm spring breezes swaying thick, heavily perfumed lilac branches, and the sense of being safe and admired by approving grown-ups nearby.

My brief time in Włodzimierz was happy and carefree. I was just a little girl and loved using my fanciful imagination. Red and yellow hollyhocks swayed outside my bedroom window. A nasturtium peeped from the garden where a furry bee had crawled into a flower and become stuck. Soft, bright waves of reflected light rippled and shined in our pond.

My cousins and I would play by the fence that was densely overgrown with thistles. In the heat their red flowers and prickly leaves gave off a sickly-sweet smell. Sometimes the smell of wet grass hung in the air. A cuckoo would be calling and rustling in the early morning mist, before a peaceful sun rose and warmed the earth. Clouds would hover in the huge, boundless sky--lazy and puffy—true Ukrainian clouds over a wild field, and its dusty, intoxicating aroma.

Pavel, the house handyman, was my favorite person in the world at this time. He infected us with his love for provincial Russia that used to be home. He knew it inside out—its fairs, monasteries, country estates, customs, and traditions. He boasted of visiting Lermontov's birthplace, Fet's country house near the horse fair in Brody, and the battlefield at Kulikovo. Everywhere he went he had elderly female acquaintances— former schoolteachers or minor local officials—who would put him up for the night. They fed him fish pie and cabbage soup, and in return for their hospitality he taught the old ladies' canaries how to whistle a polka or gave them presents of superphosphate— adding it to their geraniums would produce huge scarlet blossoms guaranteed to amaze their neighbors.

Our house straddled the line between town and country. It had been built in the early 1900s in the outskirts of Włodzimierz, the periphery of the center, where houses gave way to small rural cottages, patches of garden, and dense forest. The property was large, including a large lumber mill, the carpenter's shop, and storage warehouses. The house was the first brick house in Włodzimierz and a curiosity for the locals, who would drive out in their *droshkies* on Sunday to behold the latest construction wonder. It was very large, the windows bigger than usual, and the roof attracted special attention, as it was made of gleaming German copper.

Our house seemed gigantic. I thought its chimneys touched the sky. It was golden in the sun and mysterious in the twilight. It stood proudly amid the calm and silence of a mixed gravel and long stone road.

Had I been allowed to walk down that path alone, I would eventually have reached open country, where meadows dotted with conical stacks of hay heralded the autumn harvest. Further on lay fields, followed by brush and dark, tempting hills, and woods that stretched to the horizon.

My grandfather Jacob came from a family of rabbis and merchants—a union of ancient piety and savvy capitalism. Since Jews were not allowed to own land, he worked in the lumber business, managing the accounts of Russian nobility who'd lost interest in overseeing their forests and hunting grounds in Volhynia.

Alcohol and gambling debts eventually forced the nobles' estates to be "sold" to Jews. The word is in quotation marks because Jews were not actually permitted to buy land. Seeing a window of opportunity, however, Jewish accountants and business people *were* able to buy up logging and shipping *rights*, and become timber merchants, using log lumber to build wooden furniture, tables, beds, wardrobes, chairs, cradles, and coffins.

By the 1890s, our family had in this manner come to own or manage thousands of acres of forestland in Volhynia stretching deep into Russia and the Dniepr River country. Because of grandfather's prominence in the lumber business, the family had in fact joined a tiny Jewish elite given honorary citizenship in the Russian Empire and exempted from certain restrictive laws that applied to the broader Jewish community.

By the start of the twenty-first century, the family's sawmills and forests employed many Jewish and Ukrainian timber cutters. The workforce was international—Polish, Russian, and German, depending on the project. Workers felled pines, assembled them into rafts, and poled them down the Dniepr toward Kiev, where sawmills turned them into lumber for Russian industry. Grandfather was officially appointed by Tsar Nicholas II to build steps for public buildings in St. Petersburg as well as supply ties for railroad construction. His business flourished; he was awarded the medal of Timber Merchant of the First Guild of the province of Volhynia and granted citizenship in the Russian Empire— a rare honor for Jews.

Złoczów is first mentioned in chronicles of the fifteenth century. It had a population of 30,000 when I lived there between the two world wars, roughly divided among Poles, Jews, and Ukrainians. In contrast to Włodzimierz, which developed under Russian political and cultural dominion, Złoczów entered the modern age under Austrian influence. A part of the Polish Commonwealth until the partitions of the late eighteenth century, Złoczów remained in the Habsburg Empire until it reverted back to Poland after World War I. Some Jewish residents were Złoczów's intellectuals and Zionists. In the 1930s, many idealists left for Israel's cities and kibbutzim to work the land. The town became part of Soviet Ukraine after World War II, and now Zolochiv is part of independent Western Ukraine.

My grandparents Mendl and Chana lived in a fancy brick

apartment with a wrought-iron balcony in a building in Złoczów overlooking a park. I played with my toys as I sat on that second-floor balcony and watched people in the street below. The building was near the market section of town, which later became the Jewish ghetto.

When visiting them for summer, I recall going to the local photographer's with my cousins. I still have a formal photo wearing a children's outfit styled like a naval officer's uniform, with a coat made distinct by a double row of gold buttons.

Grandfather Mendl was a wholesale merchant supplying the Polish army, while Babcia Hancia (as Chana was known) helped him negotiate contracts and keep the books. He was arrested by the Russians on charges of being bourgeois and sent to Siberia, where all traces of him vanished.

Babcia Hancia, a businesswoman, worked in the warehouse with Mendl every day. She was friendly with all the suppliers and the two army purchasing officials, and gifted them with products for their own households.

Through a miller, who became the middle-man, she was able to negotiate with a local farmer to construct a bunker beneath the barn in Podhirce, a nearby village. She negotiated for a sum of five gold coins every month. The Nazi horror followed, in which half of Europe's Jewish population was murdered, among them more than one and a half million children, including my younger brother Janek.

2

THE WAR

MY JOURNEY BEGAN as a child in the late 1930s in Włodzimierz, when my parents provided me with a stream of denials and obfuscations about the terrible events we were living through. I remember that food preparations, household tasks, and social events suddenly became less important than the inlaid, dome-shaped mahogany "magic box"—the Telefunken radio in the study that crackled, whistled, and sputtered with bad news and became the focus of adult interest. I picked up ominous and threatening war chatter in Polish, English, and German, and strange-sound-ing names in languages my father and uncle both understood and feared, names like *Anschluss, Atlee, Chamberlain, Stalin, Churchill, Sudetenland, Czechoslovakia,* and *Russia.*

Hitler had marched into Czechoslovakia, and Poland was next!

Another war was imminent or already happening. My father and his brother continually argued about what they were hearing. Father's eyes, always serious, became more and more frightened as, in trembling hands, he chain-smoked Polish Dwusetki cigarettes.

My uncle Shlomo was calmer and more composed, reassuring his younger brother with stories of their father's experiences with the Germans in World War I, not so long before. The Germans were orderly and cultured, Uncle insisted. Their soldiers and officers behaved like "gentlemen." After all, Grandfather Jacob had been awarded a military cross for his army service.

The sparkle in Mother's eyes had vanished too, and she was upset and anxious. Still, smiling and loving, she insisted that all was normal. She was afraid to be so far away from her own mother in Złoczów and said we would move to

Grandmother's apartment in Galicia for a short time. Of course, as always, I could take my books and toy animals. She reassured me that we would have lots of fun and go on vacation to a real farm where I could feed the animals, perhaps learn to ride a little horse, and swim in a brook. Surely we would be back home in Włodzimierz by autumn, when the "unpleasant disturbances" would be over.

Looking out the window in my room, I watched a hole being dug in the garden for our silver and jewelry, and the linens and china counted and locked up in cabinets.

The caretaker helped my parents pack up two trunks and many valises. Tears, kisses, and good-byes were exchanged with the family we were leaving behind and would never see again.

In September 1939, Hitler and Stalin attacked and divided Poland, with the Soviet Union annexing its eastern provinces and Western Ukraine. When Germany invaded the USSR almost two years later, in the summer of 1941, it occupied Złoczów—but not before the retreating Soviets massacred all the occupants of the local prison. Soon thereafter, Ukrainians went on an anti-Semitic rampage that lasted for three days. Three thousand Jews were murdered. At the same time, the Nazi authorities, together with the Ukrainian police, drove the Jews into the ghetto or systematically deported them to labor and death camps.

My father, a civil engineer, was put to work for the German army, the *Wehrmacht,* reconstructing war-damaged bridges and roads. He worked in that capacity until my mother arranged for his escape by hiding him in a hay wagon.

In September 1942, my family's situation changed again. The German army's defeat at Stalingrad was a turning point in the war. As the Soviets began their inexorable march toward Berlin, Poles and Ukrainians realized that the Germans were not invincible. Despite impending defeat, however, the Nazis kept rounding up the Jews for extermination camps.

That summer we fled to Złoczów. The rapidly frightening reality hit when Hitler proclaimed *Judenrein* in Poland. *Aktionen* (hunts for Jews) periodically followed. For my safety, my mother arranged for me to live in a Christian house as a fake "cousin." Soon neighbors informed on them, though, and two Gestapo agents stomped into the farm house, looking for a Jewish child. One of them tightly held a growling German shepherd on a leash. The big dog sniffed around, while the other agent smiled and chatted with my "aunt" about the hot weather as I held her hand.

He plopped onto a chair, asked me to sit on his lap, and playfully bounced me on his knee. I was cool, smart, pretty, and instinctive enough to know danger. And he knew he had found what he came for and was satisfied.

I told him that I was the family's Polish cousin, Zosia, and that my parents were away working in an arms factory in Saarbrücken, Germany. He played along with our make-believe game until, after several minutes, which seemed like eternity, he got up and left me sitting there bewildered.

My mother came and fetched me from the farmhouse, and from there we went to Podhirce, where my parents, two other family members, and I went into the bunker beneath the barn. One bucket of food a day came down, and one bucket of waste went up. Occasionally the farmer's wife would take me up into the barn, so that I would be able to see daylight through cracks in the wall and breathe relatively fresher air. I also remember Nazi boots stomping overhead in the barn, when my father put a pillow over my head so I wouldn't make any sound.

I was luckier than my little brother, Janek, who was a toddler and might have cried in the bunker, imperiling all of us. Babcia Hancia took him away to a "safer" place. Soon enough they were both murdered, as was my entire extended family.

I was seven when I entered the bunker, nine when I was liberated by the Russians in June 1944. Only about a hundred Jews, among them six children, survived out of about fifteen thousand in our small town.

The farmer's family who saved us were "righteous Christians," but they had an agenda. The agreement was to hide us for five gold pieces each month. Since, in a small village, everybody knew everybody else's business, they couldn't spend the money: the Nazis would execute anyone hiding Jews.

So as the war dragged on and months passed, the farmers became more frantic and made plans to kill us themselves. We only learned of this plan months later, when they told us the story after getting drunk at a party to celebrate our liberation—and theirs from the fear of hiding Jews.

I have always wondered about this plan, because they talked about killing the adults but not me. What would they have done with me?

More than a million children were murdered during the Holocaust. The few that survived were hidden in convents, orphanages, haylofts, and sewers. They are hidden children, and I am one of them. With my Jewish identity and Polish cultural roots, the primitive hostility of Poles and Ukrainians destroyed the world I viscerally remember. I don't think an outsider can fully understand this condition: a carefree childhood traumatized and stolen by the war. My perceptions and memories are ragged.

A litany of hurts and abuses became grieving memories of the Holocaust—the murder of my toddler brother and a large extended family in Europe are the phantoms strangling my life with anxiety. Remembering can be like dreaming, and when memories are fearful or threating, I often fall back on illusions to manage.

More encouraging adventures with Russian culture and language began in July 1944, when we were liberated by Russian soldiers and were able to leave the bunker under the barn. After interminable days of gunfire and the rumble of trucks down the only road crossing the village, an eerie quiet settled around the farm. No barking dogs remained, no stomping boots, no Germans shouting commands to farmers to expose Jews. The Russians continued coming, and with them came singing and dancing, accompanied by happy accordion music. We survived and were liberated! A tattered 1945 Russian poster still hangs in my office eight decades later. The poster depicts a tired but triumphant Russian soldier, rifle pointed, marching through bombed-out Polish cities and Ukrainian villages for the motherland, marching west toward the Nazis' final surrender in Berlin. Glory to the soldiers who saved us from war, reads the legend on the poster, beside an unfurled red flag with a hammer and sickle.

My parents, cousins, and the farmers celebrated in the farmhouse with music, food, and lots of vodka. "Let's drink to our motherland, to Stalin, to the glory of Russia! Hurrah!" A soldier offered candy, gently took me in his arms, tied a red pioneer scarf around my neck, lifted me onto a table, and loudly ordered me in Russian to repeat his words: "I am a young pioneer. I am Stalin's daughter, defender of the USSR!" Although my father was uncomfortable with the communist dogma and the Marxism, it was the only time I noticed his approving beam! I had little understanding of what I was saying, but this gathering was the happiest, kindest, and most memorable experience since we began our two years hiding in the bunker.

Our small family travelled to the Czech Republic after the war, and then to a displaced persons camp in Germany. An American uncle then found our names on a list of Holocaust survivors and, two years later, brought us to New York City.

It took me more than half a century to tell the story of this devastating childhood. It has only been since raising my own family, and the passage of years, that I have felt secure enough to cope with the past.

Remembering my childhood in Poland (now Ukraine) is no flight of nostalgia, because I can only recall places where I endured fear. Like all Hidden Children, my ruins are unlike any others. The best example I can give of a monument to our grief is the Janowska site near Lvov: This memorial depicts a woman reading to a child whose head has been cut off.

Nevertheless, the more time passes, the easier it becomes for us to navigate the chaos, carnage, and murder we witnessed. I survived by becoming a silent human being for almost two years in a bunker under a barn, forbidden to utter any sounds. I was terrorized by noises—Nazi boots hunting their prey above my head. I was their booty, to be tallied among the six million.

Father, Mother, and I managed to survive the war; whether we survived our wartime selves remains a mystery.

3

DEGGENDORF

WHEN WE REACHED the displaced persons camp in Germany, our family was given a separate small space they called an "apartment" in a barrack that had formerly housed the German Air Force, the Luftwaffe. We were unusual among survivors because we were a *family*—not intact, but still a mother, father, and child. We were in Deggendorf, in the American Zone, where the American soldiers didn't know what to do first for the thin, pale, and frightened people they encountered.

Europe was still in turmoil: spouses looking for each other, parents seeking children, children trying to remember who their real parents were. People were waiting for days at railway stations, waving photographs at those arriving from camps. Cries of *Have you seen my husband? My child? My mother? My father?* echoed throughout Europe's bombed-out railyards.

What seemed like a world of refugees packed the camp. There were Hungarians and Russians in better shape than the Polish Jews who had returned from concentration camps, Jewish men who had defected from the Polish-Russian army, families from the Soviet Union. Many survivors from other cities and towns in Poland, like us, showed up daily.

Our accommodation was luxurious compared to what we'd endured in the bunker. The beds were wide, the sheets white, the mattresses springy. A night table with a reading lamp stood beside each bed, and a small iron stove, with lots of stacked wood, provided heat.

We had green blankets with *US* stamped on them, pillows, pots, pans, and cooking utensils for our portable benzene stove. They were all of first-class quality. My father always said that the Germans knew how to make the best of everything. Mother made sure she collected all the necessary extra cooking utensils—a meat grinder, a wooden mixing bowl, and a sieve (*drushlak*) for noodles.

The JOINT Distribution Committee helped people like us. They issued a small, badly tuned upright piano for the lessons mother had asked for me. I also got an excellent two-wheeled German bicycle from a local warehouse where there were lots of German skis and small boxes of postage stamps with Hitler's face on them. When the American soldiers accompanied us to the warehouse, they'd grab a handful of stamps and throw them up into the air like confetti. They encouraged me to do the same, but I was still too afraid.

The U.S. Army commissary distributed all the basic staples, including cigarettes, raisins, thick chocolate bars, tea, coffee, and canned peaches (an exotic fruit we had never tasted), American condensed milk, American ground anchovies, American powdered eggs. We brushed our teeth with American toothbrushes, swallowed American vitamins, and my father took to chain-smoking American Camel cigarettes.

Besides the canned peaches, chewing gum was also new to me. I got plenty of it from the American soldiers, who chewed gum a lot and showed us how. "You have to chew, but never swallow or you'll choke," one explained. "It tastes like peppermint leaves. After a while it stops tasting, but you can keep it in your mouth until nighttime. Then you stick it someplace until morning, so you can chew it some more."

"I chew it like the Americans do," I boasted to my friends as I bit down hard for a few seconds and created a wonderful little crackling pop. I was proud of this new American peppermint experience. I knew about food that I had to chew before swallowing, but this was something new. I put all five pieces of gum in my mouth at once and chewed and chewed the big ball of greenish-gray stuff, then saved it for the next day to chew again.

The refugee camp also contained a common room with an American ping-pong table and card tables. Near the common room was a dispensary, what we called "the sanitarium," a veranda with wooden deck chairs and bright artificial lamps with which the children were irradiated. I was allowed to lounge on a deck chair and listen to American music on the radio. "You Are My Sunshine, My Only Sunshine" was my favorite song.

I began to reconnect with what seemed like very distant pleasures, and riding that bicycle truly became an adventure, almost a madness, of freedom from confinement in the bunker. The Displaced Persons camp was now friendly and familiar, the only place, for me. My soul began to lift as I peddled faster and faster through a nearby park, and then the frenzy of release swept me into a profound calm as I gazed at the beauty of the paths and the flower beds, the ponds and willow trees. Still another event tamed the existential rage. Frau Sontag came to teach me piano twice weekly, which I hated. One time after piano lessons I carelessly stuffed the oven with more wood, and instead of practicing, ran out to ride my bicycle, causing a minor fire in our apartment.

4

EMIGRATION

Uprootedness and exile are among the central literary subjects of our time and culture. Coming here from a war-torn Europe, I almost immediately adopted a bi-cultural identity: how to speak and write and be myself in a splintered, challenging language while still tethered to, and dealing with, horrific and terrifying events across the Atlantic.

It is July 1947, I'm standing at the prow of the ship *S.S. Ernie Pyle,* watching the water tear away in a diagonal, forever repeating, forever receding line. The ship, operated by the U.S. Military Sea Transportation Service, was our ship of hope. Built to transport three thousand soldiers, it carried fewer than six hundred displaced persons from Bremerhaven—only a hundred and fifty families (units of more than two), many aged, and sixty-three orphans.

I talked a lot with my father about the history of continents and oceans. I saw the vast blue seas between Europe and America, and I knew I couldn't just skip over continents. Still, I never grasped the enormous distances, and never understood the cultural and emotional expanse I was about to cross.

My grandmother had also told me that, when Jews were supposed to cross water, the waves parted miraculously. But the waters of the Atlantic did not part for us. I was on a huge boat, and there were no miracles. Even in the bunker under the barn, my feet had been planted on firm ground. I had been programmed to run, to flee and change location, but there at sea I was cast adrift and dependent on the course of the ship, trapped by the perils of the open ocean. No *Aktionen* here, only the open sea and sky.

I feel that my life is beginning. We are leaving the Holo-

caust, the bunker in Podhirce, Ukraine, Poland, Czechoslovakia, and Deggendorf behind. I am almost thirteen, and we are
emigrating! It's a notion of such definitive finality that, to me,
it might as well mean the end of the world. I am clutching my
mother's hand wordlessly. I hardly understand where we are
and what is happening to us. My parents are highly agitated.
Of the place that we are going, I know nothing: New York,
that famous place where Uncle Isaac lives. It's not too far from
Delancéy Street (as my mother used to say). We are going there,
rather than Israel where many of our refugee friends have
gone. As the ship pulls away, the foghorn emits its lowing sho-
far sound, but my being is engaged in a stubborn refusal to
move. My parents put their hands on my shoulders, consoling;
for a moment, they allow themselves to acknowledge that
there's also pain in this departure, as much as they wanted it.
At that age, I felt that I had left the natural world I knew, and
I've been pining for it ever since. Despite memories of wartime suffering and daily struggles to survive, I still felt that I
was being pushed out of a familiar safety net. I had lost much
extended family during the war, as had all the other refugees
in the Displaced Persons Camps in Germany. I had to cling

to my mother, who'd repeatedly saved our lives during the war by acts of physical and emotional strength and sheer wiliness, and who was strong and sturdy enough to save me now.

For days, there was nothing but the sea and sea sickness. The Atlantic is mostly gray and not beautiful in this early July, but it's so immense, so without end, that it makes me anxious to contemplate all of it, and I have to concentrate on the manageable straight tear on the water's surface. I don't know what's come over me, but I find it difficult to keep still, and I don't want to stay near my parents any more than I have to. I fight with them and stalk off in fits of stubborn sulkiness.

There is nothing dull about exploring the interior of the ship, and its two dining rooms. Although seasick and heaving most of the journey, I tasted exotic fruits I'd never seen before—olives and bananas and even a pineapple for dessert. There was also a group of kids who every day met in the lounge or around the Coke machine. There was Lila, an authoritative figure among us, because she was older and because of her evident strength and good sense. Lila's parents had been killed during the war, and she had grown up in an orphanage. Now, she is being adopted by some distant cousins in Boston whom she has never met. She was facing her new fate with a kind of open-eyed stoicism. She was a good student, and she wanted to study physics at the university; that's exactly what she'd do in Boston. She'd let her cousins help her for a while, but she won't be dependent on anyone.

Then, there was Marek, the central magnet drawing me towards the group. He was also older, about sixteen—and he had dark sandy hair that fell over his forehead in a strip, and a nonchalant manner that included smoking cigarettes with a great deal of deep inhaling and ferocious stamping out in the ashtray. Marek had grown up with his mother, about whom he spoke resentfully. I gathered that she was an alcoholic and had not been kind to him when he was a child. He's going to Boston as well—to join his father, whom he has never seen; his father left Poland during the war, before Marek was born. In Marek's mind, the father stands for everything that is great, exciting, and good. It will be "capital"—*capitalny*. He had promised to go fishing with him, near an old pioneering outpost called Cape Cod.

Emigration had become of the most vital importance to me. All the processes of uprooting, transportation, replanting, acclimatization, and development took place in my own soul. After retiring, I sense the wonder, and the joy of my small garden, expand into the dimensions of peace. My professional and emotional life had always been rushed. The purpose was not only achievements, for even after I attained them, the need to keep moving forward was never satisfied.

I am beginning to sense no rush; passages of time becomes more restful. What are we running to, indeed? As my father would ask, "For what is the purpose?" Good question.

My vulnerability, so undefended, has led to a kind of strength. I have known how to be powerless, but with time, I don't allow myself to be blown about helplessly. Traumatic experiences in America have left wounds that probably can never be healed. Although many times I've had no control, I've learned how to use my own will, how to look for symptoms and root causes before sadness or happiness overwhelm me.

Patiently, I use English as a conduit. My interior language has become English. I dream in English, and I assimilate the external world in English. I see where the languages I've spoken have their convergences.

I have allowed myself to trust English and to say what has

so long been hidden and touches my most tender spots. Perhaps any language, if pursued far enough, leads to exactly the same place. In English, I wind my way back to my old, Eastern European nostalgia. Full awareness of ourselves always includes the knowledge of our transience and the passage of time. With that knowledge—not its denial—things gain their true dimensions, and we begin to feel the simplicity of being alive. It is only that knowledge that is large enough to cradle a tenderness for everything that has been lost—a tenderness for each of our moments, for each other, and for the world.

It is only within a human context that the world can become loved and known. I look at the flowers; some of them I've never seen before; some names I've read in botany books but haven't put together with the flowers themselves. "Azalea," I repeat. "Forsythia, delphinium." The names are beautiful, and they fit the flowers perfectly. They are the flowers, special flowers in my own garden in New Jersey. Their brilliant colors are refracted by the sun. This small space expands into the dimensions of peace. I breathe the fresh spring air. This is the place where I'm alive. How could there be any other place? I am here now.

5
AMERICA AND WASHINGTON HIEGHTS

FOR US, HAVING ESCAPED from war-torn Europe, New York was bewildering, strange, complex, and unexplored. The clattering tempo of its life—big, unstoppable streets flowing with people and cars, the asphalt, sidewalks, the lights, the billboards, nothing stood still. Life was running at full speed. In the distance, giant factory chimneys sent up smoke.

For a moment I felt that the American "Susan" who'd come off the *Ernie Pyle* had been left on the docks, and that the old "Szanka"—who felt off-center, didn't speak the language, dressed in her American nylon dress and hand-me-down clothes, carried her green loden coat over her arm, and didn't know about life in America—had reemerged.

"This is the United States. Life here is very important, very important," my uncle said, and I giggled and laughed for the first time since I disappeared into the bunker.

Uncle Isaac went to find his car while we waited and waited with our baggage. It was endless for an impatient child. Finally, he returned with a very large gray Buick, and we packed in. I was squashed in the front seat between Isaac and my mother, trying hard to formulate my first American sentence.

"Is this your taxi?" I finally asked hesitantly.

He smiled and explained, "Here, the yellow-and-black cars you see are called taxis, and they carry passengers from place to place. This car is my own. Americans can work hard, make money, and buy things that belong to *them*. America is a country of opportunity. I worked for my Buick, bought it for dollars, and it belongs to me. Here, it is no disgrace to work hard. Workmen and capitalists are equal. Everyone is called 'you' or 'mister,' and everyone goes to school. Education is free. Light is free. Music is free."

I felt comfortable in the car. I had come on wings of irony and fate, the winds of happenstance, and the backs of American machines. I leaped and ran and climbed and crawled, determined to unravel the tangle of events that would make up the first breathless years of my American life.

We drove to a place called Washington Heights. This neighborhood, a prestigious location originally populated by Jewish immigrants fleeing Hitler in the late 1930s, consisted of blocks of gray stone houses with serious facades and small courtyards of neglected plants. The air was heavier as well. But where were the ponds and willow trees and paths I had sped around on my bike in Deggendorf?

We took an elevator up to the apartment; it was my first time in one. The furniture in the dining room had already been moved aside to arrange for sleeping space for us. Made-up fold-away beds were ready. There were no closets, though, and we would have to share the children's bathroom. The dining room table had been pushed against a wall, where Rebecca suggested we put our suitcases. I was introduced to the twin Imber girls, Abby and Michal.

Since I was five years older, I was told that, in time, I could take care of them. Surprised, unhappy, and uneasy, I felt suddenly demoted from the center of attention to caregiver while still so desperate myself for love and attention.

Isaac and Mother were emotionally excited. My father sat motionless on a chair. We waited a long time for dinner, and I was disoriented and hungry. The kitchen was too small for seven, but we squeezed in more chairs and at last sat quietly for a tasty repast. I was happy to see familiar food. I recognized the meat loaf (a long *kotlet*), familiar and delicious potatoes, and strange green vegetables looking like cooked cucumber.

Aunt Rebecca was a social worker, an ardent Zionist, and not terribly welcoming. Each morning she questioned my parents about why we had preferred America to Israel, where she believed all Jewish people should settle and work the land—a conundrum to me: If that was the case, why was Isaac's family in Washington Heights?

She did take me shopping once and bought me a one-piece gym suit in dark blue, which served as a playsuit in the hot weather and as the start of my new American wardrobe. I wore it all summer.

6

WILLIAMSBURG: THE DRIGGS AVENUE GROCERY

AFTER A FEW WEEKS WITH Uncle Isaac, HIAS found us an apartment in Williamsburg and, with distant American relatives, financed a small store for my parents just down the block—the Driggs Avenue Grocery.

Mr. Seltzer, who was soon retiring, agreed to sell the store to my parents with the understanding that he would stay for a while and teach them how to run the place. It was a six-and-a-half-day-a-week enterprise. He taught them how to take inventory, how to negotiate prices with food salesmen, where to display the freshly baked goods and "three-for-ten-cents" bagels, and when to run sales on beer. My parents were over-whelmed by the language, the customers (who were mostly Puerto Rican and always asked for *cerveza fría*), and the sales-men who descended on them like a swarm of flies. Many of Seltzer's old customers needed to continue their credit and pay once a week, though the salesmen wanted, or possibly needed, their money right away.

My parents were overwhelmed, trying to integrate into the working-class American culture of Williamsburg, working al-most all the time in the store, understanding a little English and no Spanish. I was almost thirteen when my cousin Frieda, an American relative who helped me register, accompanied me to my first formal school, a local junior high, PS 50 in Wil-liamsburg.

Stranger in a strange land, I was eager to make friends and fit in, but my clothes were not trendy enough, my hair too curly, my complexion too fair. The teachers were welcoming and kind, but classmates didn't like me and laughed at me for my stilted English sentences, vocabulary mistakes, and poor pronunciation.

A refugee, I searched for love, safety, and acceptance but was often greeted with jokes and smirks, triggering the same anxiety and frustration I had with my father. As I couldn't please him, so I couldn't please Miss O'Connor, who always complained that I had terrible handwriting and said I would never learn.

Either a lack of concentration, or some emotional quirk (today, people would of course call it post-traumatic stress disorder, and I was certainly shell-shocked, if not by bombs, then by life) prevented my fingers from forming legible letters on a page. . .and to this day my cursive writing is still appalling.

The worst disaster came in Home Economics. Not understanding the American measuring system properly, I was never able to complete my project, sewing a kitchen apron, and got an "F" in the class.

Mother told her relatives that she knew the grocery business from her father's warehouse in Złoczów. She worked constantly, from dawn to eight at night, waiting on customers and hauling large boxes of cans, cartons of soda, and milk bottles. She managed everything. She added up the prices on a big brown paper bag with a thick black pencil, inquired about the families' health, and saw customers out the store with a big smile and a personal thank-you. A savvy businesswoman, she prided herself on not making a mistake in her calculations. My mother was beautiful and much given to putting herself together, and I was embarrassed many times to see the brassiere strap hanging out of the capped sleeve of her house dresses and aprons.

Barely a teen and abandoned, this time by my parents struggling for success, for a second life in an alien country, I regressed again but was happiest when she was able to prepare my version of comfort food—spaghetti, cottage cheese, and ketchup, which I ate alone in the back kitchen.

Robbed of a childhood, I gradually realized that I was nearly as helpless and isolated as I had been in the bunker. Was this America, the Promised Land, and my new life? The New American Susan was being completely marginalized by the grocery business.

Father was a civil engineer and had been a well-to-do professional before the war. He complained of phantom angina pain and constantly rubbed the left front side of his work jacket. He manned the tall, threatening steel cash register, taking cash or credit, and studied English by reading a newspaper with a dictionary at hand. He wanted to work as an engineer in New York but was too depressed to look for a job. He sat in a chair near the cash register, haunted by phantoms of life before the war—work in Volhynia, his staff, the family, his German car (a 1930s Opel), the lumber yard, orchards, and forests. He often said that a "catastrophe" had forced him out of Ukraine, where his condition had been diagnosed as melancholia.

My sense of helplessness and anxiety resurfaced. In the bunker I had been the focus of my parent's lives; after liberation and in Deggendorf, I was again the center of our refugee acquaintances but still very much in need of love and a sense of affection, tenderness, and protection. I became a deprived and envious kid, jealous to the point of envy and anger at my cousin Dina's devotion and care for her toddler daughter (Dina and Buma hid in the bunker with us).

Williamsburg was a foggy bottom devoid of nature, possessed of dull and dirty sidewalks and faded yellow-brick apartments with gray garbage cans under the stoops.

I was stuck in the doldrums of junior high school then—

taking Home Economics and sewing classes, too proud to sign up for commercial courses like typing or bookkeeping. I took the academic course but could make no sense of American history or literature. I was confused by Mark Twain, Robert Louis Stevenson, and "Hiawatha," and baffled by the Brooklynese spoken around me. I was isolated in the dreary two-room apartment. I'd sit moping and sullen on the front stoop, or hang around the store.

We were, as we had been before, itinerant refugee travelers displaced to yet another strange Promised Land.

I gave up competing with the grocery store, beset by constant frustration, disappointment, anger, and irritation. My parents were stuck there while their peers were already restoring their *petit bourgeois* lives in Kew Gardens, in Flatbush, or on the West Side of Manhattan, with one child studying in a university there, and another already accepted at Stuyvesant High. Some families had already moved to the Garden State of New Jersey.

What about *my* new life?

I felt deep nostalgia for our refugee camp in Deggendorf, where people had been friendly and accepting and exercised familiar body language, and for the happy and amusing American soldiers.

I missed the DP campgrounds and the park where I could peddle my bicycle around a beautiful lake and glide under willow trees, along precise and well-groomed paths and past flower gardens. There, my parents' refugee friends had paid attention to me and my accomplishments. All loved watching me master the bicycle. I had been universally admired—a special surviving child, accomplished and smart.

In Williamsburg, I was an angry outsider in a strange place, competitive and ashamed, longing for affection and recognition, and envious of Mother's refugee friends making good in America. We had no extended family, no family dinners, no get-togethers, and no cousins or cousin-club parties.

Thus dispirited and lonely, a teen with hormones raging, my only escape to freedom and adventure was the bicycle. Pedaling to Greenpoint, just the next neighborhood, created excitement—as did discovering the East River, almost in my own backyard!

I was dazzled and surprised to see water and the Wil-

liamsburg Bridge not too far away. What a thrill and inspiration—a gigantic structure dangling high over the water, a fine
and delicate etching: silent, calm, peaceful, serene. On my
shore and estuary, there were no whizzing cars, rumbling
trains, bustling passengers, or bus exhaust fumes.

Instead, I had found the natural world I so longed for—
my private escape, my oasis, with green grass, wildflowers, and
strange tall green reeds poking out of huge stretches of water
with silent waves, dirty patches of sand, and a small beach. I
pedaled there often to think about my world and destiny.

Only a nickel bus ride away, I imagined a different world:
the Lower East Side and Seward Park High School. Crossing
the bridge was to be my escape from life's dreary routine in
Williamsburg! I dreamed of new American experiences, new
friends, upward mobility, and real life-changing achievements.
Imagine: a "greene cousine" less than three years in America,
striving for a better social life with new action in new surroundings.

Acceptance by peers came slowly with new teachers and
Latina girlfriends, strangers themselves. Life became more

fun. I was invited to sweet-sixteen birthday parties with risqué spin-the-bottle games and dances to strange rhythms. In Deggendorf, the only American songs I learned from the soldiers had been "You Are My Sunshine" and "Home On The Range." I was eager to hear the lindy and the jitterbug and sing Fifties juke box tunes by Elvis and Chuck Berry and Fats Domino.

My own sixteenth birthday was coming up in November, and I worried how and where to have a party. There was no living room in our small apartment. Father didn't pay attention and ignored the fuss, but Mother excitedly spread the news about our first festive event in a new country!

One of her friends offered her living room. With help from some girlfriends, the plan moved forward. A birthday cake from a special bakery. Large bottles of soda, potato chips, and pretzels. Boxed donuts. Cold-cut sandwiches!

Whom to invite? I only knew two boys, one a refugee neighbor from my street, the other a yeshiva student living in a dormitory across from our apartment house. Frightened, the yeshiva student immediately declined, but the other, Freddy Sondheimer, also a new German refugee who lived on the

Upper West Side and was a student at Brooklyn Tech, liked the idea and agreed to bring boys. Alas, only one tagged along. Freddy had already been accepted to Brandeis University, an out-of-state college far away in New England.

I sensed he liked me and was impatient for spin-the-bottle. He was also helpful in finding me my first baby-sitting job, for his young nephews. Later, waiting tables on Loon Lake in the Adirondacks, Freddy led me to my first, extraordinary exposure to natural beauty.

At parties our talk was mostly funny chit-chat, but it was also prescient. Ignorant of American or Jewish history, or of Brandeis and its sponsorship of a university education for students to whom other doors were closed, its name had no meaning for me then. But Freddy was interesting and, unlike the other neighborhood boys, he and I had Europe in common.

Our friendship opened another parachute leap: an escape hatch from Williamsburg, an out-of-state school. I had never known such places existed. Waltham, Massachusetts, was far away from Brooklyn and the Lower East Side, not in England but in New England, Massachusetts! Freddy was encouraging.

He helped with logistics for meeting Brandeis's Dean Berger, who would be coming to New York in the spring to interview candidates.

Idon't remember the subway ride to the interview in Manhattan. Though determined, I was also alone, and it was probably a terrifying trip for me.

Clarence Quin Berger was the dean and executive vice president of the fledgling school. During the war, he had served as an American army officer in Poland, liberating and saving concentration camp survivors. I was impressed by his good looks and sympathetic approach. After a long conversation with many questions, I sensed that he felt that he had discovered another young person to be saved from the killing fields of Brooklyn!

I had had no schooling at all before P.S. 50, Williamsburg Junior High. I knew no grammar, no English or American literature, little math or science. I did have some knowledge of contemporary European history and of the Polish, Russian, and German languages. My SAT scores were dismal, my grades only average, but the interview went very well. I was in the right place at the right time, and Dean Berger was en-couraging.

Freddy helped with the application. Mother wrote the $25.00 application check. But my parents remained cautious and uneasy about the huge expense. How could they afford $600.00 for tuition each semester—$1,200.00 for room and board, plus my personal allowance? This was an extraordinary amount of money they couldn't manage. City College in Man-hattan, by comparison, was free! And they were overwhelmed by losing me to a school in strange, faraway New England.

But that spring of 1952, a letter of acceptance to the Bran-deis class of 1956 arrived. I had been awarded a full-tuition, room-and-board scholarship. With money no longer the issue but my parents' attitude still ambivalent, I was determined to go and began researching the school.

A freshman at Brandeis! How to get there? How to be-have? How to dress? Other parents must be well-to-do and paying those huge sums, I figured, so their kids must also be elegant and better clothed. I began buying the magazine *Seventeen* and read about clothing, makeup, and hair styles. Perus-ing the magazine, I decided that my looks were acceptable. I had good skin, no acne, and curly hair—OK. But my skirts, shoes, sweaters, pajamas, underwear, and a possible brassiere needed attention.

Distant relatives with a dry goods store on Canal Street supplied sheets, towels, a blanket, and pillows, all free, to be shipped from the business.

Their sister "Aunt" Frieda, a school principal, took me shopping to Fourteenth Street. Klein's, a palace with a profusion of items—blouses, dresses, sweet-smelling perfumes, leather and plastic purses—was packed with crowds, noise, and confusion. I remained focused on appropriate college clothes, which we couldn't find.

Orbach's was the next stop. There, I spotted a real-life copy of a page from *Seventeen* magazine: a yellow cashmere sweater set with a pleated plaid skirt to match! I tried the outfit on, loved the look, and, peering in the mirror, already felt that I was a genuine Brandeis freshman. Frieda hesitated, though—the set was too expensive for her budget. Determined to have it, I added my squirreled-away gift money. The shopping adventure ended joyfully.

A catalogue describing the school, academic courses, fees,

and administrative instructions, and another welcoming letter with dormitory information and a room assignment, arrived before the end of summer. The latter included my New York City roommate's name and a schedule of dining-room employment to subsidize personal expenses.

I had already been hired by Freddy's sister as the children's baby sitter for the family's summer in the Adirondacks, and with that, my impossible mission ended successfully!

But how was I to get to the school? My parents had no car, time, or resources—and were again embarrassed and ashamed. My roommate's parents offered a ride.

The going-away morning was complicated by an unusual scene. Father, dressed in a suit and Sulka tie, stood seriously and uncomfortably near the curb of the grocery store. Cousin Dina, with her toddler Doris next to her, was cheering me on. Mother, in a neat new housedress and without her work apron, moved between our store's entrance and the sidewalk, quietly crying, happy, and excited.

A Studebaker arrived, and they quietly greeted the good Samaritans. I was shocked when my beautiful roommate, Rosely, a graduate of Music and Art High School, obviously a rebel and wearing jeans, was first out of the car when we all met for the first time.

After some cordial if awkward conversation and small talk, mother dumped a large bag of sandwiches, fruit, and candies on my lap, and a store customer fitted my suitcase into the trunk. Embraces followed, tears and kisses, with repeated instructions about phone calls and questions about the school vacation calendar.

Then it was time for me to go. I opened the car door again, lingered, and was slightly apprehensive leaving my parents. I kissed and embraced them, Dina, and Dina's baby again—and jumped in.

And then we were off! I was happy and sad. My feelings of anger and rebellion eased, and the neighborhood appeared gentler. I was also somewhat disoriented.

I looked forward, though, to a new life that I could not yet fathom. The car, packed with four passengers and college supplies, was hot, tight, and unpleasant, with gasoline fumes, noisy traffic on the streets, long traffic lights, tolls, bridges, and endless roads.

The scenery, and my mood, improved in Connecticut. My

roommate's dad stopped for rests and gas, and later we went to a diner for lunch. I was happy to hide mom's brown bag in the car, just in case, as Mother worriedly advised, I grew hungry in the wilds of New England.

Driving north, the trees got thicker, the air cooler. Were the roads more beautiful? I was mesmerized, immersed in the natural surroundings. A canopy of trees let in soft shafts of sunlight from the late-afternoon autumn sky. The oak leaves seemed on fire, maples like outstretched hands. A tapestry of gold, vivid pinks, reds, and crispy autumn browns was drifting down. Some pirouetted in midair before cascading to the earth below.

My husband Eliot and I would often drive to Maine with friends, spend hours looking out at the ocean in all weathers, feast on astonishingly inexpensive lobsters—but the moments among those maples I saw on my way to Brandeis remain, for me, the most arresting.

In so many ways my life has been like my mother's. I have soldiered on, and drawn strength and courage from our losses. Competition with the grocery store for love and attention, and my dislike of Williamsburg, pushed me to find Brandeis and Columbia universities. Not happenstance but tenacity and hard work took me to AIG, Ukraine, and Russia.

7

BRANDEIS UNIVERSITY, 1952–1956

"To the students of the first twenty years, who helped give Brandeis its image of intellectual vitality and passionate concern for the underprivileged and disinherited."

—*from Abram Sachar's preface to his autobiography; he was founder and first president of Brandeis*

THE NINETY-ACRE Brandeis University campus sat on the site of the defunct Middlesex Medical School. Open fields surrounded by lovely woods offered shelter for flocks of birds and garrulously quacking mallards afloat on small ponds.

When Brandeis took over, though, the site was a natural

disaster. Roads were eroded, fields choked by undergrowth, and poison ivy grew everywhere. Founded only four years earlier, it was a university in progress, a school under construction. There were tractors, excavation machinery, and cement mixers everywhere you looked, the whining of pneumatic drills, and the occasional *whump* of distant dynamite blasts. Treacherous plywood paths ran between muddy ditches skirting rock piles.

They faced three new, half-constructed buildings. The school was expanding and growing, and I wanted to grow with it.

Reading Sachar's autobiography now, I understand that I was a real person, part and parcel of "the underprivileged and disinherited" group of young people sought out to study there.

We were assigned to a half-pie dormitory room on the top floor of The Castle, a large, curious building inherited from the old medical school. It looked, though, like a castle no architect had designed: a real honest-to-goodness fairy tale castle, with dramatic towers, spires, and balconies. We almost expected a knight in shining armor to ride through the gate, rather than new students and proud-looking parents inspecting their investment. (There was *one* such knight, a larger-than-life fellow named David Zimmerman, but while I first met him at Brandeis—he was an editor of *Justice*, the college paper—he won't really enter this story until the very end!)

Orientation was crammed with visits and introductions to the library, the medical office, sports activities, the creative arts programs, student union meetings, and future campus events students needed to know about.

Miss Lane, the campus minder of women's morals, reviewed the rules and regulations that governed hygiene, laundry, and social activities, curfews, dates, and boys' visits (everyone's feet had to stay on the floor in dormitory rooms visited by members of the opposite sex). Newspapers, and one unreachable pay phone, were our only contacts with the outside world.

My roommate, Rosely, had brought along a phonograph with many classical records. I'd brought several Picasso and Modigliani prints, which I carefully pasted on a stone wall facing the leaded gothic windows.

We were all invited to President Sachar's nearby house for a get-acquainted tea. It was the highlight event of the entering Class of 1956. Miss Lane warned us to be nicely dressed, and to wear hats and gloves. Many girls, including me, had neither, and Rosely was outraged.

In the house itself, though, a genuine welcome and attempt at informality and humor prevailed. Several professors and administrators, along with Ralph, the school photographer, were part of the crowd. His dog Chumley waited patiently on the lawn. The only formal note at the gathering were the ladies who carefully passed out small linen napkins and porcelain cups of tea.

President Sachar described the university's core mission: to promote humanist values of language, literature, philosophy, and the classics. Brandeis had a humanities curriculum of social sciences, history, literature, and natural science. The school's pedagogical task was to expose us to the best in Western thought and literature. We listened. I was confounded and impressed by the president's talk but had few ideas about the intellectual context except for the words *European and Western Thought and History*. I sensed that, somehow, I was a very tiny piece of Western civilization and needed to study its history, but I only truly understood his praises of its humanist values. I felt lucky to be among a faculty of tough individualists, quarreling and exposing intellectual battle for its own sake. But all were united against mediocrity.

My immediate decision was to study European Intellectual History and Politics, since the world was Eurocentric. Russia language was not part of the curriculum. I had loved Russian from the time the Russian army liberated us in 1944. I had learned some ungrammatical Russian from the soldiers but been criticized by Father for my clumsiness with the language.

I felt enormously lucky to be in an environment so very different from Williamsburg or the Lower East Side. And I warmed to the president's eagerness to expose us to the best that had been thought or written in the West.

The new university also broadened the opportunity for men and women to whom other doors were closed as an important visible symbol of protest and advancement: Jewish intellectuals fleeing European academic schools, or escaping from Europe during and after World War II, found a home there.

We were fortunate, truly lucky, to work with intellectual giants in our core curriculum. But we had no real understanding of the experience and their genius. As Robert Frost once put it, "A schoolboy may be defined as one who can tell you what he knows in the order in which he learned it." Give or take a few ideas, the same could have been said of us—or of most college students; eager as they may be to seize the moment and follow their fuzzy dreams, they lack a framework that only a measure of maturity can bestow on them. We were ignorant, one more instance of talent wasted on the young.

Only many decades later do I grasp how fundamentally important these great courses were for students like me. I will only mention a few that I really remember.

Frank Manuel taught Intellectual European History. He was one of the two or three most stimulating members of our faculty and a most productive and respected scholar. He rapidly became my hero and a mentor, a profound and refreshingly witty human being. He did not care much for most students. His tongue was sharp, his temper quick. His fuse was very short. Class began at 8:00 a.m., at which time he locked the heifer door. (The classroom had been redesigned from a cattle barn.) I loved class and was always on time, but late students had to enter through the open balcony and crawl on the floor to their seats, so as not to be seen by Dr. Manuel.

Decades later, I understand that his anger was tied to a physical disability: a terrible war-related calamity, the loss of a leg, and that he was infuriated by the laziness (or thoughtlessness) of young people with two healthy ones.

I felt the course would be comfortable for me because of my journeys in Europe and the events I had lived through on the continent; I sensed that I could contribute stuff about Europe to class discussions.

Instead, the course was about concepts entirely strange and unfamiliar! It went into the consequences of the development of human nature, determinism, materialism, the Enlightenment, revolutions, and atheism.

Manuel's lectures on intellectual history examined in great detail the gifts of historical realism expressed by Machiavelli, Nietzsche, Freud, Marx, Weber, and Hannah Arendt, as well as the naïve idealism of Woodrow Wilson, a bleeding heart (his racist views were still hidden then).

Sigmund Freud was an especially fascinating figure for Manuel. His work and acute insights into secular Western thought quickly seeped into our minds and drove us ever inward to confront our own experiences and understand our own interior world. We were not studying in a medieval university but palpating the history of the now and the future (what the great Welsh poet R.S. Thomas called "the fragile bones of a sick culture"). Manuel's sense of history was tragic. The concepts of national interest, the nation state, and the balance of power were long-term realistic perspectives on a cold and cynical world. The savage lessons of Munich and Hitler could not, argued Manuel, ever be over-learned.

Max Lerner was the students' favorite. Completely informal with young people and faculty, he sat comfortably on the stage and chatted about American history in a most relaxed and informative manner. We thought de Tocqueville was his personal friend. Pre-war European scholars were shocked by his display of American freedoms.

Lerner was also in the habit of chasing female students and was rumored to have had hot assignations with my roommate Rosely, about which she said nothing and I was too embarrased to ask.

Herbert Marcuse was another gray eminence at Brandeis; a philosopher and political theorist with a solidly Marxist bent, one of the pillars of the Frankfurt School, he has often been called the "father of the New Left," and he certainly appealed to young leftists among us (I leave it to the imagination of my readers to judge how much any of us actually absorbed concepts like "repressive desublimation," but his tone was unmistakable).

Then there was Leonard Bernstein, who of course had such a brilliant career as conductor and director of the New York Philharmonic and composer of some very great classical as well as popular music. I remember his stunningly good looks and his beautiful midwinter Caribbean tan. I've heard he was composing *West Side Story* when he came to Brandeis. (Lesser known to some, his *Symphonic Dances from West Side Story* has captivated me at least as much). In a black overcoat and a white silk scarf, he made his way dramatically down the center aisle of the auditorium, casting aside the coat and scarf as he came, and hopped effortlessly onto the stage. When he reached the piano, he was ready to begin his lecture. He went through different composers and operas, at times singing and playing snippets to make a point. Students were astounded, amazed, flabbergasted. A new musical world had effortlessly been opened to us! He organized Brandeis' first summer musical festival, which included Marc Blitzstein's English adaptation of the *Three Penny Opera*. (His *Young People's Concert* series, which began a few years later, and which so many people were lucky enough to attend or watch on television, followed the same scheme.)

The hiring of Irving Howe, the literary critic, was a major coup for the university because he was widely respected by both liberal and conservative intellectuals. When he disagreed (and he disagreed more often than not), his sharpness rarely cut superficially. He reserved tolerance and patience chiefly for his students, and then only for the ones who demonstrated promise. He always wrote with social purpose. He was deeply interested in Jewish proletarian life and edited anthologies that brought together the classics of Yiddish literature.

In Ukraine, we had believed our family's professional and business stature validated our assimilation. Polish had been our native language. Pilsudski in his time would have referred to us as Poles of the Mosaic faith. Culturally we had been, we thought, a cut above Sholem Aleichem's Tevye, a poor farmer.

We did not know better until Hitler and World War II. To the surprise of Uncle Isaac's family, I learned my Yiddish in America, when it became the *lingua franca* for him and other, distant, relatives and grocery customers. Only after some twenty-five years in the States, when Holocaust course studies enabled me to write my earlier memoir, did I finally grasp how Howe's course had opened a new world of Yiddish culture for me. In Howe's opinion, Isaac Balshevis Singer's older brother, Israel Joshua Singer, was a better writer, despite his younger brother's greater fame. We read his novel *The Brothers Ashkenazi* in Howe's class. I. J. Singer's critics have compared him to Tolstoy and he was mentioned as a candidate for the Nobel Prize. When he died at age fifty, his younger brother Isaac was still unknown.

In my freshman year, I was overwhelmed by my core studies—trying to read and understand new concepts in intellectual history, Greek and Latin literature, the humanities, the existential philosophy of Sartre, the musical cadences and themes in the poetry of Rimbaud and Lamartine in French class. Evenings, I worked as a salaried busgirl in the dining room cafeteria. I had no time for a social life and culture.

There was also a lot of Bohemianism among the students and experimentation with drugs and other amusements, but those same obligations prevented me from opening those

"doors of perception," as Aldous Huxley called them in 1954.
. .though I might have been too shy even if they hadn't!

It was a time of great political ferment on the campus, but for me political activism exclusively meant my escape from the Nazis. I saw myself as a Serious Student who denied herself the luxury of relaxation time with classmates—to have a beer and talk about Plato and pizza at Saldi's, the local dive.

I didn't even make time to check out the boys or be checked out by them! I was unaware of formal student balls in hotels in Boston, on-campus record hops, or auditions for *High Charlie* and other variety shows. Rosely and I chain-smoked Lucky Strike cigarettes in our freshmen year, but I didn't even know I could enter a Lucky Strike contest to win prizes! Later, petrified by a diagnosis by Dr. Pena (aka "Penis") of emphysema, I stopped smoking forever.

Brandeis University planted the seeds that grew into this memoir. The school's special character in the 1950s as a liberal Jewish bastion of critical scholarship guided my intellectual and cultural development, all of it in an age of ideological relativism and in the travails of my own struggle for self-discovery. It was an unforeseen and immensely privileged gift.

8

WHEN AND
HOW TO MARRY

IN THE 1950S, MARRIAGE WAS mandatory, almost universal, and the nuclear family triumphant. Only the "sick," "immoral," or "neurotic" preferred to remain single. Women were expected to marry as soon as they graduated college. I was, in addition, the only available beacon of hope to restore my parents to the bourgeois life.

And Mother required my husband—whoever *he* was, no ifs, ands, or buts—to be a doctor.

I was introduced to Eliot by a mutual friend. There was a folk dance coming up soon on campus, and Eliot's friend Zvi invited me. My initial attraction to him was intellectual and aesthetic, not physical. But he was an authentic medical student, the first I had been lucky enough to date.

Thus, away at college with a scholarship, I had found the man—or, to be more precise, the profession—my mother had always wanted me to marry! I was twenty, a junior, and I followed the marriage template—become engaged in one's junior year, and marry after graduation.

As scheduled, I was therefore engaged in the spring to be married after graduation, near the end of June. I called my parents with the good news that I had found my knight in shining armor, a medical student from Boston.

Eliot's father had died when he was young, and upon hearing the news of the engagement, his family was happy for him and his mother, Sally, since Eliot was struggling with medical school.

I knew nothing about the protocol of engagement and marriage in America, since I had only been in the country for five years, with my parents working all the time. The last wedding I attended, before my teens, had been that of a cousin in war-torn Ukraine.

I knew nothing either of customary preparations for an

engagement. Eliot presented me with a sparkling, pear-shaped diamond ring, and Sally hosted an engagement shower for friends and acquaintances. As gifts, the guests gave silver utensils for various uses: cake knives, serving knives, forks, spoons, *hors d'oeuvres* doodads, and crystal. A great time was had by all. Guests were glad (or at least relieved) that Eliot was marrying a nice Jewish girl, albeit a refugee and from Brooklyn. I was happy with the presents and wrote Emily Post stationary thank-you notes to the participants.

Relatives and friends coached me on how to plan the wedding. Since we were refugees and my parents were consumed by work in the grocery store, we didn't know where to begin. By default, I became my own wedding consultant. That led me to Bachrach Photography, *the* Park Avenue firm, famous for creating pictures of debutantes for the *New York Times*, and, in a flight of *chutzpa* utterly without boundaries, I engaged the company.

With help from my mother's friends, we then located a place in Brooklyn called The Manor. It possessed some Hollywood splendor.

The ceremony itself was one of a kind. People were already seated in the chapel, facing a wedding booth decorated with lace, beautiful flowers, and fruit. Music was playing. The rabbi and the wedding party took their places. And then, from the upper level, a curtain swung open to reveal—the bride! *Me!* As if the feature in a circus routine, or a modern *deus ex machina,* I was lowered into the *chuppah*!

Delighted, smiling guests exhibited suitable levels of shock and awe: how had a Williamsburg girl fresh from war-torn Europe managed to catch a Jewish doctor—and from Boston, no less?

Eliot, who was poor and still a medical student, had grand ideas about our honeymoon and married life thereafter. He reserved a room at the New York Plaza for our wedding night. I don't remember the tryst except for the shining white bed and our mutual discomfort.

We celebrated our first wedding day with a breakfast of oysters Rockefeller and champagne. Soon after, we left for Cape Cod in our Volkswagen Beetle. I had no ideas at all about intimacy or sex or, for that matter, the least familiarity with the concept of marriage. All I knew was that I had married my mother's dream. He was going to be a real doctor within a year, and she could tell all her friends and relatives that her mission had been successful.

During the honeymoon, we had fun swimming and walking the Cape Cod beaches, collecting shells, searching for antiques, and admiring the green grasses and the purple cosmos in bloom. I had never seen the beauty of the natural world as I did then, for the first time since childhood.

Also, Eliot was an aesthete and a craftsperson. He taught me how to collect shells, made a long, beautiful shell necklace for me, and, as a honeymoon present, bought a straw basket and personally—and artfully—interlaced it with blue ribbons. I was grateful for its wonderful, imaginative quality!

When we came back from the Cape, Eliot returned to medical school for his fourth and final year. I was lucky to have found work as a fourth-grade teacher in Waltham, Massachusetts, for which I was paid six hundred dollars a month. Eliot's uncle Abe, an old-time plumber and landlord who knew Cambridge (and was super-conservative when it came to money), helped us find an apartment at 115 Mt. Auburn Street, which, being near Harvard Square, was an exciting place to live but cost a hundred and fifty dollars a month—twenty-five percent of my pay. We could walk to the

Harvard co-op, the Brattle Theater, movies, and really interesting shops. Eliot's hours were long, so I had time for the co-op, grocery errands, and careful shopping. A blue cashmere sweater and skirt contributed splendidly to my future role as a doctor's wife.

I have already alluded to Eliot's ideas about the good life, and when he finished med school, he chose an internship at Greenwich Hospital in Connecticut to achieve it. We settled into a small apartment in town, near the hospital, and I again found a job teaching grade school in the Greenwich system and, after school, commuted to Columbia University for graduate studies.

So Eliot, a Dorchester boy from Boston Latin School and Harvard, was getting there!

His extended family in Boston told many stories of Eliot's adolescence: how he was the best and the brightest, and the most fun. They described his summer adventures in a New England boy's camp—the only camper or counselor to wear bikini swim trunks and show off his physique; campers would steal the bikini suits to hang on the flagpole.

9

TEXAS AND RIVERDALE

ELIOT COMPLETED HIS internship in Connecticut and enlisted in the armed services as chief medical officer for the Medina Air Force Base near San Antonio, Texas—a strategic air force intelligence operation.

I got there eight months pregnant with Lisa and our great big standard poodle, André, in tow. I was away for the first time from familiar places and faces in New York and Massachusetts. I was homesick and missed my parents and friends, my teaching life, and the East Coast. The base was lonely, unfamiliar, and strange, and I felt out of place. I felt even more estranged and different with Lisa: we were the only Jewish family on the base. Career military families, both personally and culturally, were utter strangers to me. No introductions were made, no welcome or get-acquainted parties organized. There was almost no neighborly chit-chat either, and no children's laughter on the street. Medina was a serious base, and its residents followed serious protocol.

The arid, cookie cutter-flat ranch houses resembled a landscape of mostly artificial surfaces; there were very few shrubs and little green, no grass or flowers or ponds or lakes. The air was thin and dusty, humid and muggy, the sky always cloudy, and there was no wind. Bizarre and lonely, at least for me, it was miles from the city of San Antonio.

Our new 1950s ranch house stood on the most distant housing perimeter; it had small windows, inlaid linoleum floors, and a large "modern" kitchen (for those days) with built-in cabinets, Formica counter tops and, wonder of wonders, a brand-new washing machine! The kitchen door opened onto a small asphalt patio with a sturdy metal government-issue clothesline and wooden clothespins. Beyond stretched a huge, treeless, and dusty back yard.

I had never seen such a housing plan or construction in

America or Europe. It was American design for the American desert, though it wasn't easy to imagine cowboys and Indians in that landscape. But looking at nature from there was interesting anyway, since the yard abutted open fields and prairie, on which grasses grew and some cropland was being worked.

Eliot spent his days in the infirmary. He had a lot of free time. He filled it by hand-hooking a purple-and-white wool rug. He befriended many air force pilots too and spent hours flying. We took road trips as well to national monuments and tourist hotspots on the West Coast, and spent time in Nevada, Santa Fe in New Mexico, Colorado, and the Grand Canyon.

I was surprised and anxious when my water broke one late afternoon in December. I panicked, and André whined. I telephoned the infirmary to discover that Eliot had left for the day, only to remember later that a pilot buddy had invited him to fly that afternoon. I called the emergency line, and the MPs arrived at the door almost at once. André barked furiously seeing his police friends, a *déjà vu* moment for him.

They drove me in a hurry to the nearby Lackland Air Force Base hospital. Nurses were pleasant but had little empathy for me, an anxious and frightened woman admitting herself without a husband in tow, alone in the new Texas world. "First time for y'all, honey?" asked an older, well-endowed nurse with wavy blonde hair tucked under her starched cap as they were escorting me to a room. "Where you from? Where's hubby?"

"Out flying, but he should be here soon, any time now."

"Our men love their planes better'n wives, we all reckon!" she declared, shaking her head.

I was in pain and smiled silently.

A long and excruciating twenty-four-hour labor and difficult delivery followed. I tried to control my cries but couldn't; I was terrified of needles, as frightened of lumbar injections as of the birthing process. I was already sedated and pushing out baby Lisa when Eliot arrived. It didn't matter, of course—1950s protocol barred him from the delivery room.

Flowers, phone calls, and two gift parcels came. Eliot's family congratulations decorated window ledges in my room, among them an extraordinary bouquet of birds of paradise in a crystal vase, very unusual and exotic, from my husband.

Soon enough, though, I was home alone again with baby Lisa and post-partum depression, overwhelmed and sleep-deprived. I was mono-focused on diaper changes, the diaper pail, and the near constant noise of the laundry machine. And there were the feedings too, and bottle scrubbing and sterilizing. I was sad and cried often, and I had no one to talk to about any of it and imagined that other young mothers routinely breezed through these chores and that there must be something the matter with me. When I strolled around the base, other housewives would peek at my daughter, curious to see whether she had horns instead of ears.

"Where did you get *that* idea?" I asked one of them in astonishment when she actually asked.

She thought about it and shrugged. "Musta been in bahble class at home, or my grammy or church," she finally said matter-of-factly, brushing back a strand of her lank blonde hair. "Well, thank the Lord she is nohmal—and *so* enchanting."

I may have been isolated at home, but Lisa was a beautiful, happy child who enjoyed playing with the dog and scooting around the house and yard on the newest toddler contraption: a walker.

I couldn't control André, though. He was young and powerful and bigger than me, and he often escaped. He loved running around the base, covering vast distances, picking up ticks, and often humping stranger's legs. Neighbors constantly complained, and the dog was frequently hunted by the military police, many times caught and locked up until Eliot "freed" him.

Eighteen months later, Jonathan appeared. We were thrilled but unaccustomed to so much crying. It was impossible to comfort his colicky tummy. I was helpless—and exhausted by his discomfort. Neighbors suggested native potions and medicines. None proved effective until I discovered a miracle drug: a bottle full of sugared chamomile tea! It brought relief for Jonathan and much-needed sleep for his mother.

Two years after that, my exile in Texas came to an end. (I don't know what else to call it, though I recall Ernest Hemingway writing, of places he had worked in, "Some were not so good, but maybe we were not so good when we were in them.")

We returned for Eliot's residency at Montefiore Hospital in New York with two small children and the dog, and rented an apartment in a two-family house in Riverdale. I walked my menagerie to a large park across the street, where the kids had fun and the dog, nostalgic for the Texas prairie, ran unleashed. Domesticity, care of children, and dog walking became my life's work.

I again felt unhappy and dissatisfied—until Eliot found a reliable baby sitter and suggested that I return to graduate school at Columbia University's Harriman Institute. I tried to do double duty but couldn't. Responsibilities at home and classes in Russian literature and history were exhausting, and I was grateful to catch up on a little sleep in class and do the reading at home.

I was infatuated with the alliterations of nineteenth-century classical poetry, struggled with Old Church Slavonic and Greek and Russian linguistics and with the cadences, intonation, the very texture of the words great poets from Pushkin to Akhmatova and Brodsky had written.

Highpoint on the Hudson, a very classy apartment building in Riverdale that was home to many Montefiore physicians' families, was our next move. We couldn't afford a river view and settled for an apartment facing the street. But Highpoint was *paradise!* We were happy and comfortable.

The building housed many young families with friends for the children. Eliot began making more money working house calls at night for patients in the Bronx. I monitored the telephone, relaying messages from a medical exchange in the central office. We were self-employed, operating a cash medical-exchange business before the cell phone was invented! We were grateful for our sense of comfort and well-being. Imagine! We were near New York City with money for a full-time baby sitter and tickets for an occasional concert or play!

That same year I was hired by the Bronx High School of Science as a permanent substitute teaching History and Russian. I loved the school and was energized by the students as well as interesting colleagues. I liked the work and wanted to continue teaching. Then the huge budget crisis reared itself in New York City just as I was applying for a permanent teaching position—I had scored first place in the New York City History examinations—and I lost my job. It was Murphy's Law operating to create a bureaucratic nightmare.

But being hired as a permanent substitute teaching History and Russian had brought me one step closer to my future, though I had no idea it would at the time.

10

LEARNING
THE TRADE

WHAT TO DO NEXT? Luckily, the Nixon and Kissinger détente with Russia came along and did the trick. I was hired by Chase Manhattan Bank as a market researcher for companies interested in Russian business. My first opportunity, as a translator and interpreter, was to travel to Russia with a non-ferrous metal dealer named Mr. Filner, doing business in Moscow through a company he had founded called Noblemet.

Filner, an aging 1930s American communist nostalgic over the ideology, did not speak Russian and needed a translator for negotiations. I was young and ambitious, a genuine Russophile with graduate degrees in Russian language, history, and literature, in love with Russian culture, fluent in Russian, and excited to be hired by him.

I had no business experience whatsoever. I was illiterate in finance, geology, and non-ferrous metals. My boss seriously mentored me, though, and I was resolute to master something about trading and earn the round-trip ticket to Moscow. Filner taught me the ropes about doing business in Russia; he was a godsend. As I have said, I had nothing but a graduate degree in Russian Literature but, in him, the tutelage of a gifted and generous boss.

In the 1970s, before the digital revolution, Filner's small platinum-group metals trading office functioned with one secretary, three telephones, two tape machines, a telex, and me—the Russian-speaking gofer.

I shopped with and entertained "visiting colleagues" and "officials" of the Russian U.N. delegation (all of course actually KGB agents) with fancy lunches in high-end New York restaurants and costly tickets to the Metropolitan Opera and Broadway shows—all on Mr. Filner's expense account. Luckily, he liked both the opera and Broadway, so I got to accompany him as his date.

As a result, I quickly became a liaison between the Russian State's nonferrous metal agency outpost in New York and Moscow.

Our Russian counterparts were intrigued by this Ukrainian immigrant before them, and a woman no less, in such a prestigious if undefined position in an American company. My nickname was *"Zolotaya Susanna.,"* "Golden Susan." They loved the personal attention I gave them on both continents: I was resourceful, understood their sense of humor, and almost become the American equivalent of the new revolutionary, liberated Soviet woman!

Within the time he needed to secure a Russian visa, Filner succeeded in pounding enough information into me about all that, as well as negotiating contracts, to make our Moscow trip a success. The Russian State agency counterparts loved the American version of the smart, modern Soviet woman (me!) in action.

Our Russian counterparts must have been excited vetting my dossier. They'd have seen I was almost Ukrainian-Russian, had survived World War II as a hidden child in Ukraine, and that my father had graduated from the Kiev Polytechnic Institute University on that miniscule Jewish quota. I was therefore more European than American—almost a *landsman* (*zemlyak* in Russian), a native.

And there I was, bright and civil, attractively enough turned out—some kind of a fugitive academic, a lover of Russian history, culture, and literature. I wasn't a consultant, not really an associate, or for that matter in possession of any corporate designation or title; I wasn't a lawyer either—just a postgraduate student in Russian Studies doing commercial research on Russian resources and employed by Chase Manhattan Bank.

The Russians must have figured that I was a spy disguised as a researcher whom they needed to keep an eye on.

Imagine, a lover of literature turned corporate shark staying in a spacious, elegant room at the Hotel National in Moscow with an embroidered coverlet on the bed and a marble bathroom. I swept through a luxe lobby surrounded by exquisite marble columns and the glitter of gold statuary, headed for a high-level meeting elsewhere. Spring is more a state of mind in that city. It's a burst of electricity running through you that you feel, the sense that you can and will accomplish great things. I tried to convey some of that sense in the novel *Norilsk* (Full Court Press, 2013). Mr. Filner and I certainly did make great achievements on that trip—the first of many I made thereafter; and I began to reach deeper into my nature, into the deep recesses of my heart, and find rare powers there I hardly knew I had, though I had always felt their distant strength. I will, I suppose, always be flying along a path by a lake on my bicycle and feeling that wind in my hair.

I was so self-involved that I truly believed my charm and intelligence had been instrumental in Filner's successes! We celebrated many events with our Russian counterparts, sharing champagne and caviar toasts around the white piano at the Bolshoi—and, curiously enough, met Henry Kissinger there, another fan of the Bolshoi Ballet visiting Moscow.

We laid on the food and wine pretty liberally in those days at social events where, upstairs at the buffet tables, Communist Party hacks were stuffing themselves sick with state-subsidized caviar, smoked salmon, sturgeon, and cream cakes; when they thought no one was looking, they grabbed ten more sandwiches and stuffed them in their briefcases to treat their families.

Mr. Filner introduced me to his long-time friend Sergey, a KGB cultural attaché who had been assigned to "mind" me. He was cultured, attentive, very handsome, and he insisted I find the time to take the overnight train to St. Petersburg, Russia's cultural capital, to see the ballet and the Hermitage. He said he would be honored to make all the travel arrangements and reservations at the Europa Hotel (the most elegant in town) and for seats at a performance of *Bayadere* at the Kirov Ballet—including the red-carpet treatment for a backstage visit.

Sergey was a charming and solicitous companion. He tried very hard to seduce me in a classic, sophisticated European manner. I loved his attentive style but knew better, sensing I might be fresh bait for *kompromat* (which sounds almost suave but means "compromising material" employed as one of many varieties of blackmail), and graciously kept my hormones under control.

11
CHILDREN

I CAME HOME TO PREPARE Lisa and Jonathan for pre-school. Both had circles of friends in the building by then. But even as children, their interests diverged. Lisa, always curious, was interested in adult conversations and reading; Jonathan was very active with his little buddies, rough-housing in the pool, playing "army," and flying off swings imitating superheroes like Superman and Captain Marvel (landing himself in the hospital).

I persisted in feeling, however, that merely to be a doctor's wife, albeit a very special "working doctor's wife," was not enough for me. Unusually for a woman in the early Sixties, I wanted it all. Hooked by that first Russian trip, I was ready for business challenges without attending business school. My ego struggled with ambivalent views of professional achievement and baking cookies. I didn't, quite simply, know who I was.

Back home, we remained a stereotypical young doctor's family: well dressed and mannered, intelligent and respectful. My templates were the Kennedy children. I wanted my kids to look like Caroline and John, and I dragged them to an upscale discount store in Brooklyn for classy clothes. Jonathan did not complain and never paid attention to what I bought for him. Lisa was recalcitrant. I forced her to try outfits I liked and bought, which she hated. She was very beautiful and very smart. As a kindergartner, she was already reading and involved in adult conversation. Jonathan had difficulty competing with his sister's talents and curiosity.

Truth is, I was unconsciously following my mother's 1930s European model for raising children, which was long on observation and distant tough love—and no physical touching or play.

Following this petty-bourgeois model, the mimes of my parents and Ukrainian nanny, I did not spend enough time nurturing. I did not breast-feed the older children. I loved them, I was devoted and a little overly protective, but there was not enough touching, holding, cuddling, or kissing. I never told them, "I love you." I now deeply regret my ambivalences about mothering.

My kids of course did what all kids do: They grew up.

In high school, Lisa resented my need to control. No longer complacent, she started to rebel, though she always maintained the image of a perfect student and daughter—brilliant and highly personable. At Harvard, she became a true rebel. She changed her name from Lisa to Liza, and she lived in Courier House, the same dormitory as Caroline Kennedy.

She had many boyfriends. I always made sure my parents never spent time at our home on the weekends Lisa came to visit. She came with Joe, a well-mannered, Irish-Catholic Harvard basketball player a foot taller than she.

After Harvard, she studied the history of science at Cambridge University and was interested in an academic career, but Eliot insisted she study medicine for a better financial future.

She became a well-known forensic psychiatrist in Washington, D.C., the author and editor of psychiatric medical texts, a clinical professor at Georgetown University, and president of the American Academy of Psychiatry and the Law (AAPL).

Jonathan's journey was different. Smart, active, and popular in high school, he fell in with the wrong crowd of boys at Tenafly High School. After two years there, we sent him to the Loomis Boarding School for Boys. At Loomis, he excelled in English and Social History, and he loved lacrosse and popular music. Visiting him there, we met his girlfriend, Sandra, and liked her.

We were pushing him to study pre-law in college and pursue a career in the law. He was not interested. Eliot suggested a public health field, where he could help his father in his radiology practice. Jonathan did help Eliot manage the practice but was not interested in a public health career either. Instead, he graduated from business school and now has a doctorate in business management. He has been successful in the camping industry and is president of the National Camping Association; he owns three children's day camps in New Jersey and loves his work. He's an internationally recognized speaker and writer and has become an authority on quality management in camping, speaking frequently on both the local and national levels for profit and non-profit camps.

His life's work is a sublimation of Peter's tragedy, I have always felt, and of Jonathan's love of children. For many years, he loved to watch over his younger brother at overnight camp, and there was an intense bond between them. Jonathan built his success from these experiences.

After many decades, now in my final innings, I am able to retrieve these difficult and painful emotions. I am not without deep regrets, though I readily admit that nobody interesting gets to be over forty without them. I was, as I have already said, ambivalent about mothering and often paid scant attention to the kids' emotional needs. I was selfish and narcissistic, believing that it was I myself who needed to be loved.

Our dysfunctional relationships have mostly backfired. The extraordinary power of losing both Peter and Eliot radically changed our lives. The three of us are each tethered to our anguish, but our grief and sadness have been too dangerous for engagement.

Each of us has always needed to be loved, but we've been unable to grieve together and have had to cope with those untimely deaths separately. Still, as time passes, we have begun to inch closer. After decades of resentments, angers, estrangements and alienations, I hope we are a work still in progress.

12
HOLLYWOOD ON THE HUDSON

THE TIME CAME, AS IT so often does for people who live in New York, to think about leaving the city for a place where we could be more at ease, and the kids could grow up with fresh air and good schools. We poked around some and, across the George Washington Bridge in New Jersey, eventually discovered the town of Tenafly, founded by the Dutch in the 1640s as "Tene Vlay" ("Willow Meadow" in English), a beautiful place in a valley.

We bought our house there in the late 1960s, when Tenafly was lily-white, Germanic, orderly, and very *gemütlich*. They held an Oktoberfest celebration in town, with lots of Bavarian music, yodeling, and German beer. In the '40s, the German Bund and their sympathizers had flown the Nazi flag from the middle school. A few Jewish professionals, and one Negro family, had trickled in over time.

Our wonderful colonial house had been modelled in the late '20s in the Dutch idiom—wooden beams, rough-hewn sandstone facing the front lawn and street, a well-cultivated southern-exposure back garden filled with flourishing flowers. (I remember the zinnias and delphiniums and hens-and-chicks ground cover). I called the house my "Hollywood on the Hudson."

Eliot's plan for the garden sold him on buying the house, as he was a plant expert, having also studied botany and land-scaping at Harvard and at the Boston Arboretum.

Peter, our third child, had been born in 1967. We were happy. Tenafly was Paradise, our dream. Camelot. Our wide street was filled with very old trees and broad lawns; it was a brief walk to the center of town.

We walked everywhere, in fact—to the movie house, the hardware store, the Tenafly general store, and Bower's pharmacy. As a respected young doctor's family, we had charge ac-

counts in all the small businesses. The town had an excep-
tional school system and library. The children loved school
and their various activities. We had two cars in the old garage,
and a full-time nanny, Yvonne, for little Peter and the older
kids.

Eliot's radiology practice in the City was growing. I—unusually still for a doctor's wife in those years—commuted there
to teach Russian and History at the Bronx High School of
Science.

But, alas, our neighbors were not happy. They disliked us
and hyperactive André. He often bounded out the front door,
sniffing, and, with tail wagging, relieved himself strategically
next door on Mrs. Kelly's lawn just as I tried to catch him. She
was an older, gray-haired woman with a gawky frame and a
mouth that curved downward, and she barked, "Your animal
is dangerous, undisciplined, and trouble here! Chasing cats,
squirrels, and cars, digging up flowers, leaving poop everywhere, and that recent vulgar scandal—humping little Emily
Huber!"

"Yes," I confessed, "we too were shocked when the police
came to our door."

"That fancy dog of yours is a menace—he's good for Park Avenue, not here," an officer said.

"We're terribly sorry! A dog trainer will be working with him next week. The dog doesn't know that he isn't in Texas anymore."

"That dog is a menace, and our street hasn't been the same since you people moved in!"

Mrs. Kelly and her younger, plumper niece, who was living with her, couldn't stand Jews and was afraid of us and our dog. (The beer garden too had a connection with the German-American Bund, with Hitler, and with anti-Semitic persecution of various kinds. It was hardly a unique phenomenon in Bergen County.)

André was smart, though, and he understood that neither the children nor the nanny could handle him or deal with the mayhem he was causing. But for better or for worse, with regular exercise, the trainer's work, and discipline, he soon adjusted to the leash and he lived to a ripe old age.

Our neighbors continued to gossip anyway and complain about the "new people on the street." It was a very slippery slope.

Eliot, busy with meetings and negotiations in the city, rarely came home for dinner. I shopped, prepared, and cooked after work, and each evening the children and I gathered at the kitchen table. Weekends, when he was home, my husband was super-active, busy bathing and grooming the dog, or planting and gardening, or preoccupied with laying an intricate French quarry tile floor in the kitchen. Sometimes he was away antiquing with friends, on the hunt for antique furniture and rugs. He was the man I needed, one who knew how to care for and repair the old house, and I admired his competence in all things.

"Will Daddy be here for cuddling tonight?" Peter asked routinely.

"No, not tonight. Maybe tomorrow, but for sure Saturday. He told you so himself."

But life remained beautiful, though Eliot and I were in the middle of Paradise but not part of it, at times unaware of each other's presence. I believed we were incomplete without each other and needed to stay together.

We were, however, *socially* together but emotionally in different worlds. We each needed the other to confirm us as a suburban family, but we led parallel lives and were pretty blind to each other's physical or emotional needs. I was invincible but felt incomplete without him. My own smarts and professional accomplishments were irrelevant—to me, my parents, or my children. Only Eliot's professional stature and career mattered, as a model specimen of class on its way up.

Weekend dinners at home glittered with new local friends, relatives, or interesting city people grateful for a weekend escape to the suburbs. I am thinking especially of two men who visited often.

The first was George, mysterious and endearing; he was a physician, a pianist, and a bachelor by profession. He and Eliot often traveled to other towns on the hunt for antiques and returned with some lovely old rugs. Once they spotted an old Baldwin piano they decided to buy on the spot. This stately instrument found its place opposite the fireplace in our living room. We entertained guests who were surprised by, and appreciative of, George's mastery of Brahms and Beethoven piano sonatas.

George also spent a lot of time with the children, taking them to cultural events in the city—especially Leonard Bernstein's Young People's Concerts (I often wonder how many people can claim to have both seen him talk about music and sent their children to do the same).

My nostalgia for piano lessons resurrected my mother's dream for children to study the instrument despite her memory of the "fiery" piano in Germany.

Many years later I shipped our piano to Lisa's home, without her approval. She was furious and sold it.

The other guest, Costa, was the most creative and exciting. Christmas and the *Nutcracker* were his favorite times for visits. He opened the world of ballet and theater for the kids. Before leaving for the performance (dressed as Uncle Drosselmeyer), he retold the ballet story and improvised the sugar plum dance for us all.

In real life, Costa was a professor of ancient Greek and Latin literature. He insisted that Eliot take time in his busy schedule to study Greek dancing at the Greek Club in Manhattan.

That summer, our family vacationed in Israel and returned by ship via Piraeus, the ancient port of Athens. Eliot and I were both interested in Greek and Roman history, Thucydides, and mythology, so we were excited and fascinated by his plan for our detour there, especially for him to immerse himself in Greek dancing. Costa's local friends would teach him the *hasapiko* and *pendozali*.

Costa and his friends were waiting for us as we steamed into port. He hugged us and welcomed us with flowers and salt, and the shorter of his friends strummed a very old *santouri*. Both men—well-toned, manicured, chiseled—resembled Greek statues, except for their suntan and oily skin. The very tall one waved his massive hands in the air. "This is Dmitri," Costa whispered with a sudden note of gaiety. I restrained myself from clasping them.

"Welcome!" Dmitri declared. "I have no wife, children, or dogs," he told Eliot. "I will be your slave. We create a family relationship, eat, drink, and dance together. Costa has told us about your wife and children, and I have been anxious to greet them."

Costa's eyes were twinkling. "Dmitri's old job was to oversee schedules for cruise ships, but he's an expert on the old history. He knows every nook and secret of the port and Athens, and we are *lucky* he's our slave."

Boatman porters carried our valises up a winding street to a high-end hotel on the village side nearby—a perfect picture postcard of Piraeus: white oleanders blossoming, fig and carob trees in bloom, ancient stones, whitewashed stucco houses, and red roofs facing the sandy seashore.

We passed a quiet afternoon on that seashore, with waves that didn't break but left a small coating of foam on the sand. Beyond, the noble port stretched out jagged and proud, and further on, mountains were visible in the mist. A soft sunlight infused the afternoon with a delicious tranquility.

The next day changed my life forever. Eliot vanished with Costa's friends for a very long lunch while the kids and I shopped for souvenirs in the *plaka*. After a while, the children, exhausted by the heat, tired and grumpy, needed a rest. We returned to our agreed-upon meeting place, a small *taverna* near the market, and waited. The afternoon sun glimmered on some old ships in the port. In the distance, off to the right, rose a low ash-colored mountain, treeless. The sky was darkening, with a cool, damp wind and airy clouds passing quickly overhead. We waited for a very long time.

Eliot returned much later than he was supposed to, pulled up a chair beside the kids, smiled, and hugged them.

But he seemed fatigued and panic-stricken.

"Where were you?" I asked in as even a tone as I could manage.

"We, uh, we lost track of the time," he replied with a shrug and a lopsided grin, and ordered an ouzo. When it came, he drained the glass in a single gulp.

I was startled, bewildered, and confused by the blank expression in his eyes that I knew was not being brought on by the ouzo. I was his wife, I told myself; we were an intact couple. I was in my forties. I was hot and needy and upset about his delay and our domestic scrimmage.

I felt a lack of interest, affection, and intimacy—felt it acutely then and there, and maybe for the first time was unable to bury it again as I had done for. . .well, I realized, for decades.

And I was certain I could not compete with the mysteries of Hellenic culture, with Costa, with those two male slaves. I had sensed alienation many times before, but there in a strange, exotic place, I couldn't ignore it. Too many emotions were swirling around me. Time stopped for me in that cozy, old *taverna*. I felt portents of disorder, a quirky rumbling in my gut. But I did not want to dive into unanswered questions.

More than anything else, I was staring mutely at a profound inequality of competition. I was the odd man out—and I use that noun more than colloquially. I had lost my central position and its collateral perks—the good life and privileges of a young doctor's wife in suburbia. The detour to Greece had plunged us into a dark fairytale. A train wreck was inescapable and still to come. Both of us were petrified by his leap into the unknown.

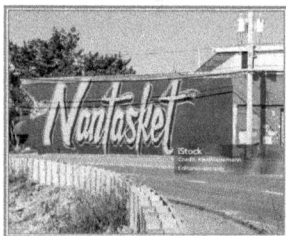

13
NΛNTΛSΚΕΤ

Maybe the shock, the dislocation, of what happened in Piraeus would have derailed a more conscious marriage than mine in those distant days. Today, decades later, the chances would probably be much greater that one of us, or both, woke up. Eliot and I managed to keep going—principally, of course, by enabling his homosexuality to again sink beneath the surface of our reality, or, more precisely, by shoving it down. Neither of us was prepared for, capable of, any other resolution. Later vacations remained lovely, memorable, and fun.

The kids looked forward to visiting our family, the Kellem

cousins, on the Hull Peninsula south of Boston. Our dog boarded, suitcases, beach paraphernalia, and other stuff packed, and the kids excited, we drove off on a historic sea change from life in Tenafly.

Vacationing to see family in Nantasket for a week and, later, a month in Truro, on Cape Cod, were more wholesome and memorable by far than Hollywood on the Hudson diversions at home. I was captivated, it is certainly true, by Eliot's witty, cultured, and theatrical friends, but I had been increasingly ambivalent about their visits. Surely, I thought, it would be easier and more comfortable to enjoy family life with the Kellems.

The trip east was long and tiresome. We took many breaks for bathrooms, and for hamburgers and French fries, with Peter's never-ending drum beat from the back: "When will we get there? How much longer will it be?" To deflect these repetitive, annoying questions, Eliot was calm but wistful, nostalgic behind the wheel. He was, after all, the prodigal cousin, a Dorchester boy transformed into a young doctor returning to visit family, ready to entertain us all with stories about his life and adventures when he was a boy.

Heading south from Boston, I could smell the ocean and feel the sea breeze immediately upon turning off the highway heading for Hull.

"Every Irish or Jewish youngster around Boston," he said as the car sped along, shadows from the clouds flitting on and off his face, "every one of them wanted to be treated to the thrills of a summer—even a day—at Paragon Amusement Park. New Englanders called the place the 'Marvel of Fantasy.' It compares quite favorably," he assured me, "to the 1930 World's Fair exhibits."

Arriving in Nantasket, we parked the car and took the ramp leading to Paragon Park.

"Imagine," Eliot enthused, "I was lucky enough to spend whole summers here! I saved enough money to follow my cousins for rides on the wooden roller coaster or jump for free carousel rides, and play games and win prizes! Oh, the smell of sticky pink cotton candy, the irresistible taste of beach pizza and steaming hot dogs!"

"How did you manage all that, Daddy?" Peter asked.

Eliot put an arm around him and studied his face for a

long moment. The breeze carried the sharp scent of kelp and salt a few blocks away. "Well," he finally said with more than a hint of seriousness, "I had to work for my money. My mother and I lived with Uncle Abe and Aunt Goldie in Dorchester, and the whole family spent the summer in Nantasket. I had a job stocking shelves at the deli. Later I was an errand boy, delivering stuff on my bicycle. I collected some pretty nice tips from customers, by the way—they were well-heeled people. They thanked me with those tips for being prompt and polite." He smiled at the distant thought. "Sundays were especially good, I'll tell you. Every Sunday I earned more than two dollars!"

"I wish I could earn more than *my* allowance riding a bicycle and having fun," Peter murmured quietly while Eliot went on explaining Nantasket's history and geography.

"A peninsula's a stretch of land surrounded on three sides by water." We were by then strolling down Nantasket Avenue, and Eliot pointed out stores that had been there for many decades and that evoked so much of his impoverished childhood. "The Plymouth Pilgrims first set foot here in 1621. You've heard of Myles Standish and the Indians in school, I bet."

"Sure I did," said Peter. "And the Indian princess Pocahontas, and John Smith, and Thanksgiving—we learned all about that in Mr. Wescott's class!" Peter shouted, suddenly cheerful and in good spirits. He was interested in the holiday, Indian weapons, and how they stuck small fish into the holes they dug to plant corn.

"That Pocahontas must've been something else," Jonathan drily remarked. "They didn't have underwear, did they?"

"Oh, be serious!" Lisa warned him. They were both dressed in khaki shorts and white polo shirts. "It's a very inspiring story—even if nobody knows how accurate it is. I read in American history that hundreds of Pilgrims starved to death that first year, before the Mashpee gave food to them and taught them how to farm."

"Mm," I said. "But sometimes, maybe the actual facts don't matter as much as the feeling behind the story."

"Very true," Eliot said. "The feeling, Peter, is always what counts!"

The name "Nantasket" is derived from Wampanoag and means "at the strait," "low-tide place," or "where tides meet," as Hull is a peninsula. Nantasket was settled not long after Plymouth Colony and before Massachusetts Bay.

The place had been settled as a seafaring village on the Peninsula near the town of Hingham. During the American Revolution, it became a military outpost.

"Remember that old big black cannon in the town park?" Eliot asked me.

"Yes, yes," I said.

"Well, that old cannon was the first line of defense for the city of Boston during the Revolutionary War."

By the 19th century, steamboats were making three trips a day between the town and Boston. Boats ferried people from Boston as well to their summer homes on Hull—famous Bostonians like Calvin Coolidge and the former Boston mayor John F. ("Honey Fitz") Fitzgerald, the grandfather of President John F. Kennedy.

After World War II, Nantasket became a summer resort area settled by prosperous middle-class Boston Jewish families who headed south to found a summer vacation community. Each summer they flocked there by the thousands, helping to turn the place into one of the most popular Jewish seasonal resorts in New England. For that ethnic population, living in crowded apartments in Dorchester and Roxbury was difficult. The older generation tried not to remember anti-Semitism and pogroms and felt nostalgic about breathing the fresh air and tramping in the fields and forests near *shtetls*. Their children, Boston businessmen and tradesmen, were eager and proud to buy land and build the large summer cottages spacious enough to settle a family in for the season. The extended families came too, for the proximity to relatives, trees, grass, yards, and flower gardens, and the healthy ocean breezes near rejuvenating waters steps away from the ocean.

The community had soon developed its own social and commercial infrastructure: a butcher shop, a fishmonger's establishment, a grocery, bakeries, and delis, as well as small antiques shops with enclosed porches, where customers negotiated over porcelain, glass vases, and decorative bric-a-brac for tables and cabinets.

The Kellem family looked forward to our stay. Larry was a small-town lawyer, and Cynthia an English teacher at the high school; they had three kids (the norm for the time), and a parrot. The two boys had successfully followed Larry into the law; and there was Amy, who came to fame and good fortune as a mortgage broker but who succeeded even more much later, when she had her family—her daughter got engaged to a medical student!

But our stay in Nantasket with our cousins was exciting for all of us. Besides Peter's adventures with Uncle Abe in Paragon Park—they took boat rides and went fishing—I especially remember the picnic table, built around a tree that Peter climbed on while we devoured lobster, beer, and French fries for lunch. Jonathan made his own impression, setting off New Jersey-imported fireworks.

Larry was unnerved by these firecracker tricks and not ashamed to say so. There ensued a few minutes of awkward silence with a chastened Jonathan avoiding all human contact amid the cracking of lobster shells and the mingled aromas of beer and butter. Lisa was, by contrast, a low-profile child invariably busy reading, and she paid little attention to her cousin, who didn't much care for Lisa anyway and tried to be the best and brightest on her home turf.

Kellem family life was what we'd have described then as

"normal integrated," whatever that meant, probably that most of everybody's time was spent with family activities, though there were the occasional private forays walking with Cousin Cynthia on which we discussed our interests and poked around antiquing in town.

Uncle Abe's private treat was the highlight of Peter's summer vacation—the wonderful, homey, honky-tonk that was Paragon Park. They both looked forward to hugging each other, eyes smiling and sparkling. But as a God-fearing Jew, Abe looked away when whoever was with them bought the boy a treif hot dog.

Strolling the boardwalk hand in hand, Peter was overwhelmed by games, bumper cars rides, the merry-go-round, and the variety of prize games to choose from. Once, he even had the thrill of winning a funny white teddy bear by throwing balls to hit the target.

Paragon Park, which opened in 1905, was often compared to the World's Fair. Through the 1950s, steamboats, trains, and famous hotels brought millions of visitors to Hull, making it one of the area's premier tourist destinations. During the latter part of the 20th century, Hull was ardently re-establishing its links to the past, while growing and prospering, as more people discovered that jewel of the region as a place to visit or live in. It offered an exciting journey through an area rich with historic hotels and beaches, maritime and military history, technological advances, and proud residents. Gamblers, pickpockets, and confidence men followed the crowds onto the boardwalks, so Paragon Park was created as a safe place for those seeking amusement.

The Park was like a time machine that moved forward and back—a blend of the new and classic, with a bright beer hall, an old-fashioned candy stand, tried-and-true New England seaside foods, games new and old, tacky amusements, and timeworn bars just across the street from the ocean and the long line of waves rolling in under a powder-blue sky.

Now the boardwalk amusements are gone, and only a few rag-tag, beer-soaked bars remain—and some fading memories of romance, of good times we may never experience again except in our haunted dreams of youth.

Early evenings with children offered exciting times for us at Jake's Restaurant on the Bay; we also enjoyed the lobster dinners and steamed clams, a walk after dinner for ice cream, and sunsets on the water—both our families were competitively focused on children and their schools, and especially on men's careers. Yes, both I and Larry's wife were working hard teaching and raising families, but always our work was marginalized, dependent on the men's professional success.

The one and only time we went out without the kids happened when we dined at a high-end restaurant and bar in Hingham to watch the Apollo landing on the moon. The first time I heard the words "That's one small step for a man, one giant step for mankind," I felt a profound sense of patriotism run through me that I knew I was sharing with many millions. It was one of the most memorable of American moments in my life.

None of us quite put it all together, but the Apollo landing merged in 1969, a watershed year, with many other moments of change in America.

People my age and a few years younger can all tick off the moments of that change easily enough. Many prefer to venture no further into any of it—Woodstock, Altamont, the whole 1969 hippie culture, communes in the woods, free love—all the chunks of a previous age that had vanished with Jack Kennedy's death and the Vietnam War and were breaking American History apart before our eyes.

We heard of pot too—even called it "grass" with a certain illicit pleasure—of LSD, peyote, mushrooms, and the sundry other psychedelic drugs compounded for pleasure and inspiration. We were afraid of them all but also in denial, confident that, as correct citizens with square values and children correctly raised, and our well-compensated professions—in short, as cultured and educated American citizens—we were following a wiser path. And we believed our children would follow the same path, and the same rules, we had grown up with. Not for the likes of us long hair and beards, ripped jeans, peace signs, flowers, or (God forbid) anything tie-dyed.

It didn't work out that way. Very, very few escaped unscathed from the culture wars of the 1970s.

Their generation also saw—more clearly than we ever did—that they needed to think for themselves, and that more life options lay on their tables.

We had never imagined that the norms we lived by and expected them to follow, all the endless calculation and study we lavished on Profession, on a Stable Source of Income, would ever be questioned.

But the kids, once they got older, questioned them *wholesale*. People of both sexes sought sexual release and fulfillment, for the first time in America outside Bohemian circles. But these journeys were driven by an even more basic yearning— to discover what being a free spirit meant to the soul. They were after a more meaningful sojourn on this Earth. They listened to and *memorized* Bob Dylan and the Beatles. They read, truly *read,* Thoreau and Whitman.

And they rode the waves of revolution (a much-overused word, but it so obviously *was* a violent, wholesale disruption of norms). The structural pinions of our society were also shaky then. Black and brown people clamored for their rights. So did women, and gay people, and American Indians.

We visited other relatives as well that summer, showing off our children to Eliot's large extended family, content and settled in their very own expansive summer cottages in Nantasket, with the water views, the sea air, the gracious old trees and gardens bursting with a succession of blooms. The menfolk left every

Monday for their trades and businesses in greater Boston, and returned early on Fridays for Shabbes and a relaxing Sunday.

Eliot, the returning prodigal, entertained attentive kin with hospital tales of patients and adventures with nurses. Sally's Boston Latin School boy had always been admired by relatives for his education and smarts. He was envied; they wished their own sons would follow a path into the respected Jewish professions—if not medicine, at least law, dentistry, or accounting.

I was bound to him and grateful for the serenity, ease, and rhythms of small-town life, and of the intimacy and direct human concern, and apparent affection, of close-knit families. My own had been shattered in so many ways by the war and its aftermath that I'd never seen such examples before. I was immensely curious and attentive to loving tales, and gossip, of who did what to whom—dislike of neighbors and their attitudes and complaints were a main feature of ladies' conversation *chez* Kellem.

Eliot's attitude to that extended family was, predictably, condescending. We were different—well-to-do, respected, world traveled. For him, the small provincial community was great fun for family visits and short vacations, but our *Weltan-schauung* was not the same. We were sophisticated, elitist, achieved.

I was, I thought even then, only Eliot's wife, but I loved visiting the cousins and the place; and, while I was somewhat ambivalent about the provincial lifestyle, I eagerly looked forward to Truro and the Corn Hill cottages on Outer Cape Cod, where we were going next.

14

TRURO

IN THE HEAVY HUSTLE AND BUSTLE
of summer traffic, we made our cautious way around the traffic circle leading to the Sagamore Bridge and crossed the
Cape Cod Canal, maneuvered another roundabout to Route
6, and were soon passing towns on the Lower Cape on our
way to the Outer Cape. I was struck as always by the gnarled
pitch pines, and the oaks that gradually became fewer and
fewer; this, I had always felt, was the authentic New England.
It comprised an odd congeries of elements that, to a hungry
eye, seemed to coexist peacefully (and peacefulness was my
deepest goal, whether I knew it or not): strip motels along the

highway, trophy homes in the hills, old signs that read US 6 in a font I couldn't place, and the low pine forests and beaches we caught glimpses of to the east.

We had been to the Cape many times, exploring, meandering through its tree-shaded towns, the heart of the New England countryside. We had followed winding roads off the highway, eager to get a little lost, soaking up and enjoying the distinctive look of gray, cedar-shingled homes, simply-designed restaurants, and the arts and culture that seemed available almost anywhere. We were struck even then by how little interest was paid to designing homes that departed much from the Cape Cod look—the boxes pleasingly added onto by more boxes, the cedar-shingled exteriors, the common inclination to present only modest elevations to the road rather than full frontal displays. These people were the epitome of restraint, and the result was extraordinarily restful on the eye.

Then, one day, seemingly out of nowhere, we crossed a narrow bridge into Truro—a one-of-a-kind seaside town on the Outer Cape that mutual friends and Eliot's sophisticated buddies often spoke about and recommended we see sometime.

Following a nearly treeless, low-lying stretch of land along the bayside, we spotted a half-hidden old sign pointing up a hill to Corn Hill Cottages, and turned onto it.

At the end of that winding road, we found Paradise! And a family had just canceled its reservation. Cottage #10 was available for rent!

If you've spent time on Corn Hill, you know that the atmosphere is indescribable. Perched on cliffs seventy-five feet above Cape Cod Bay, the colony of cottages offers breathtaking views unequalled on the Cape—a chance to be remembered beyond our time, glimpses of a pre-industrial age. Almost every town from Provincetown to Plymouth is visible in clear weather, and so, since all the cottages face west, are the magnificent sunsets over the water.

Truro's splendid isolation and striking seascapes have been a major attraction for artists for at least two centuries. The Corn Hill Cottages themselves were immortalized by Edward Hopper in 1930 in his well-known painting *Corn Hill, Truro, Cape Cod,* in which cottages facing the sunset seem to be clinging for dear life to high hills, depicting similar isolation and alienation to his paintings of personal life in New York City in the 1930s.

A group of Victorian-age Bostonians founded the present-day Corn Hill Cottages on that hill as a seaside resort in 1898. There is little mystery to why city folk chose that particular spot. Not only does it have an interesting history—the location is truly heavenly. Stepping into Cottage 10 was like taking a step back in time. Exposed, uneven wooden floorboards creaked underfoot. Windows outfitted with thin cotton curtains fluttered in the slightest sea breeze. . .and the sun, the sand and sea, and the very presence of antiquity, immediately spoke to me of the quintessential Cape Cod of salt farming, scavenging, and all manner of small industry. We had a kitchen, dining room, living room, and bathroom on the first floor. The second floor contained two bedrooms—a large one in front, and a smaller in back. It suited our needs perfectly.

What fascinated *me* most about Corn Hill, though, beyond the views and the sunsets, was the languishing sense of time and the sure knowledge that so many guests, and artists, had spent easy time there.

This *easiness* that beckoned to me touched me most. W.H. Auden once famously wrote that, though one can't always say why one was happy, there is no doubting the certainty that one was. I was not a happy person, as any reader of this chronicle I have no doubt can see—but I instinctively knew that Corn Hill might teach me precisely why I wasn't.

All of the cottages offered the same expanse of Cape Cod Bay and access to the private beach through the dune path down wooden stairs.

After a satisfying lunch, we descended the narrow sandy steps to that beach. Our children were happy as clams there, swimming and sunbathing, becoming expert at kite flying in the almost constant breeze off the bay—Eliot in front, Peter helping and cheering in back. The kids got buried in the sand, horsed around in the surf, and adored tramping way out on the sharply ridged flats that stretched for miles at low tide in search of seashells and the endless surprises beneath the surface of the seawater trapped in pools a foot deep.

And then there was the lobsterman pulling his boat onto our shore and offering lobsters right off the boat to boil and savor for dinner—accompanied, for Eliot and me, by a chilled Chablis or Sancerre. And I can still savor the ecstasy of cracking open the steaming lobster and devouring each minute bit.

I, a West Ukrainian Jew with no access to the ocean or the Baltic Sea, had only eaten lobster once before in my life, on a drive to Maine with a classmate, before I encountered it again in Nantasket. It astonishes me to this day, though of course there's nothing astonishing about it in this wide world.

Occasionally, we had an evening barbecue on the beach, the kids chasing fireflies and watching for shooting stars. And we'd head some evenings to the drive-in movie theater in Wellfleet, and sign up during the day for ranger-guided activities along the nearby National Seashore beaches.

And when the inevitable urge came for more excitement, crazy-busy Provincetown was only a few minutes up the road—the place for whale watching, dune tours, harbor cruises, museums, shopping, and tons of great food. For many, it was— still is—the town of last resort on the Cape, where outrageous dress and manners are casually tolerated. (I was struck, though, by how Eliot acted the very image of a family man in P-town—no acting out, no eye contact, no signals between him and any of the men.)

It was all truly lovely even if, as I have said, I was not a happy woman at all. There was plenty of time to read in Corn

Hill, on the porch or on the beach, and I gave myself up to Henry Beston's *The Outermost House*, which had been published in 1928 and inspired the creation of the Cape Cod National Seashore, and even more to Henry David Thoreau, who had written *Cape Cod* in the 1860s, when it must have been almost pristine and the locals did a thriving business in salvaging shipwrecks and (so he suggests) causing them as well.

But I was most captivated by the dune systems towering above its backside beaches—all visible, parabolic dunes sculpted by centuries of weather and wind, their centers scooped out as if by a giant bucket, and the sense they awakened in me of being lost and out of place. The place was magical—silent, intimate, and orderly. The awakening began in the aesthetic continuity that triggered an irresistible entry into the natural realm. I was enchanted by the way light and shadow washed the sand and the waves, and, when there were no clouds, that emptiness in Heaven as well as on Earth made me feel a deep melancholy but always tranquility as well, and peace, and repose.

It was precisely what I sought from the world, though I didn't know it—didn't, at first, even know I was seeking *anything*.

In the active presence of Nature, I have come to understand, an unspoiled subconscious is the basis of conscious perception. Everything is expressed by what remains unsaid, and so the center of gravity is not the visible but lies in ways of seeing and understanding life's shifting situations. It is possible to reach profound depths of feeling under those conditions. At Corn Hill, neither sorrow nor gravity were palpable or visible; my fantasy and imagination were, instead, validated, and they began by stages to resonate with the extraordinary beauty of the place.

The Lower Cape's loveliness derives from a practical Yankee respect for the earth, the wind, the sun, and the sea. But once you travel north of Eastham, you enter a different terrain—a country where there *is* no earth, only sand, where everything is in flux and the ground beneath your feet is moving like the ocean, only much, much slower, restrained by plants that are fighting a daily battle to hang on to it. This struck me hard, for it underscored the fragility of life, the tenuous grip we all have on it. It told me I must *live* my life, not act *as if* I was living it. Thoreau himself expressed that idea better than I have ever seen it expressed when he wrote in *Walden*, "I went to the woods because I wished to live deliberately, to front only the essential facts of life, and see if I could not learn what it had to teach, and not, when I came to die, discover that I had not lived."

My own response to the tenuous world I was surrounded by triggered a psychological transformation in me that opened my heart to the realization I must seriously reconsider my life as Eliot's wife.

To do so wasn't easy. I was an incomplete person in so many ways. I had suffered abrupt and ruthless psychological and geographical upheavals in my early years. I had lived literally in a hole in the ground for many months, hiding from people with stylish uniforms and shiny black boots who were eager to murder me. I had been left much wounded by that terror, that utter insanity—"crippled" being perhaps too imprecise a term for the state it left me in.

On the one hand, the aftermath of the Holocaust drove me to yearn that I could somehow bring reality to the personal fantasy I clung to of who I was and could be. But was that an illusion? And was it worth abandoning the unsettling promise of security I had always so hungrily sought?

My dreams were locked in mortal combat with the still-ardent wish to somehow resolve my unhappiness, to continue soldiering on with all the bells and whistles and privileges—the good life of a good doctor's wife.

The Freudian canon suggests that comfortable feelings can quite often be unsettling, and I knew in my bones that I needed my dysfunctional marriage to remain alive, a relationship with little gravity but without ambiguity—an integrated, ordered family life with continuity.

But my fascination with sand mounds and dune ridges was telling, important, symbolic, and it persisted despite my calculations: I imagined the ancient winds that constantly shaped the sands into those parabolic masses. I felt them resonating with my conflicts and struggles and uncertainties. And the hunt for tranquility remained, satisfied neither by Eliot nor by the "integrated" Kellem family.

I was more and more burdened by the *dissonance* around me—the extraordinary beauty of the place I was in, with all its inescapable simplicity, and the constant nagging absence of inner peace, clarity, or physical satisfaction as a woman. No wonder I responded so viscerally and completely to Hopper's landscapes, which seemed to me to capture the same dissonance, the same sublime beauty, and the same unsettling responses to it.

I resolved to find a unity somehow in that. It came to me that I could be invincible—that the radiance of Corn Hill could transform our family life. That didn't happen.

15
PETER

MR. PAT WESCOTT, PETER'S sixth-grade homeroom teacher, contributed the following commentary to the June 1981 Tenafly Middle School Yearbook from Memory Lane, dedicated to Peter Gold and entitled "Remembering":

"Peter Gold passed away on January 3, 1979. He was a member of our class and had attended Stillman Elementary School. Everyone enjoyed his terrific sense of humor. We

would like to remember him always as a student who was greatly respected by his classmates. Therefore, we would like to dedicate
our yearbook to him."

Peter was the shining star in our family. My life revolved
around nurturing and bonding, around being inseparable and
available. He was born in 1967, and he was beautiful: I adored
and cherished his smile, sparkling eyes, aquiline nose, and
golden curls. He easily made friends with grown-ups. I carried him as a toddler to the tennis court, where friends admired his good looks and good behavior. He just sat and
watched the game. At home he was kind, playing games with
cars and trucks in our driveway in Tenafly, allowing younger
children to win, enjoying his bike, playing soccer and baseball,
and he was popular at school.

I made no trips to concerts or the ballet, just lived with
happiness and high spirits. I stopped teaching; my identity as
a doctor's wife was replaced by the child's inexplicable radiance
as well—narcissism mitigated, I devoted myself to raising the
boy he became.

Peter was especially loved by his father and his older siblings (his "fun" set of parents).

His sudden death was my Holocaust and a permanent wounding, a bullet through the heart for us four. A venal aneurism—a severe headache at Christmas, and brain-dead in Massachusetts General Hospital two days after New Year's. It had been his first trip alone to visit his sister at Harvard, their first private time, and a great vacation—sightseeing in Boston, pizza binges, walks through Cambridge and Harvard, and Lisa and her boyfriend's present of a kitten, Tom, for entertainment in Lowell House. It was the last time she saw her young brother alive. Tom lived out his long, comfortable life with me.

When the time came to return home after that week of special fun, he complained in the morning of a headache and was given aspirin.

I had, before he left, checked all his IDs and slipped them into his new wallet (I still have it in my desk drawer), and all the logistical departure and arrival times had been confirmed. I was waiting for him to come home.

Suddenly, I received a message—early, surprising—from a hospital in Worcester, Massachusetts. "We have your son

Peter," a woman told me. "He experienced a seizure and has been admitted."

I telephoned Eliot at work and shouted for Jonathan, already home from college for Christmas break. "We've got to go to Worcester! Peter's in the hospital! You know, he's often carsick and couldn't get home before barfing!" I added in a wry aside.

The humor didn't last long. Soon Jonathan and I were speeding apprehensively to Worcester, where I was led to the intensive care unit and my unconscious son. Overcome by disbelief and shock, disoriented, I rushed to his bed and squeezed his left hand. "It's okay, Peter! Mommy's here. It's okay, okay."

I knew for sure that he had responded by squeezing back—but only once.

Hospital protocol listed his condition as stable, and I did not know better.

Three days of anguish and despair followed, of repeated consultations with doctors and a slight glimmer of hope—a possible cauterization procedure at Mass General in Boston. With Peter's ambulance leading the way, we drove through a wicked New England winter storm with poor visibility and the weather heavy and nearly horizontal, gusts shoving our car from side to side.

It ended in another hospital room, with the same life-saving apparatuses, monitors, breathing tubes. Flowers and Christmas presents from friends and relatives were there, and Lisa had already decorated the back of his bed with photographs of happier days.

But the cauterization was not successful, and Peter remained brain-dead.

A pediatric neurologist suggested we go home, rest, and return after the New Year weekend. After still another consultation and confirmation, we left for the chapel. I don't remember whether I was alone when stopped by a Catholic nurse who advised me that I had a choice—not to follow medical advice and allow my son to live. I averted my eyes and soldiered on to catch the elevator.

We held each other's hands and waited for the brutal vacancy to be resolved by machines, by nature, by something.

Peter's death shocked our community. We had sent him on his first vacation to have fun with his sister in Cambridge—and brought him home for his funeral.

There were no empty seats at the funeral service. The synagogue was overflowing with silence and grief. I wore a white winter suit. I could not feel. I walked as if in a fog; other people, pedestrians, were a human ambush. I felt utterly isolated and alone, a less-than-human creature. I remember no one from that day, not even my family sitting beside me. Seeing the coffin, I ran to embrace it and didn't want to let go. Plied away from it, distracted, I was very far from myself.

At the gravesite, I clutched white roses so tightly the thorns drew blood from my palms, which sensed no pain. I did not cry. I remained in a separate world, not so much serene as anesthetized, not feeling the torment of the burial.

That loss is a crater always close to my skin's surface—a permanent wounding. Everything that had formerly propelled me was gone. I was left purposeless and sensed small tortures and loss everywhere.

Some friends were afraid to come near the tragedy; others identified with Peter's death and found visiting too difficult. The empathetic tried to lighten my darkened world of despair and anger. But I *wanted* to be disengaged, inhuman, and they gave up.

Many months and long hours of therapy followed, endless tears of grief and anger, and painful shingles.

The first signs of pain easing came in early spring, when purple crocuses bloomed, radiant in the sun, sparkling and up-right like soldiers, but gentle and kind. My sense of grief eased, and I was able to feel an almost idle joy, believing that Peter would safely return each year as a crocus.

16
ELIOT ∧ND ∧IDS

MY HUSBAND MAY HAVE been a smart and successful physician, but he couldn't cope with Peter's death. For Eliot, it was not only a personal disaster but a professional medical failure, glaring evidence of his incompetence and downfall. He had trouble understanding me or the kids and was soon hospitalized with severe depression.

Our marriage, never really stable, could not survive that horrific loss. We were both crippled by it, still united but estranged from each other and the old life, separated emotionally by tragedy, history, friends, and family. We had unconditional mutual respect for each other and an authentic friendship, but it wasn't enough.

I don't remember when he began to drift away from the Hermès ties he favored, the Turnbull and Asser shirts and sweaters, the suits and jackets from Paul Stuart, the Italian linen outfits and boxer shorts from Harrods. He was something of a fashion plate, and he knew how to wear all of it with style and panache. Abandoning these skills by stages was not superficial, I hasten to point out—it reflected an internal hollowing out.

Eliot had always been physically healthy and active, too, even though he'd had anxiety attacks in Ibiza, and in the Casbah in Marrakesh. Whatever was going on in his head, he'd kept to himself.

After Peter's death, though, he was often ill, sometimes seriously. Within weeks, he suffered a transient ischemic attack (TIA), a minor stroke. He discounted the event and assured us that it had been brought on by stress and "not to pay attention"—that he was okay, that what he had was nothing serious, and he compared himself to New York Mayor Ed Koch, who was already back to work after a similar minor stroke. I trusted and respected my husband, and I believed in his medical judgment and expertise.

Still reeling after Peter's death, we sold our old and comfortable suburban house, filled with books, antiques, and circus posters in Peter's room. The older kids were already on their own, and the two of us banging around the place were making Peter's absence unbearable. The suburbs, and Hollywood on the Hudson, had in any event never been Eliot's thing, much as he doted on his projects and antiques expeditions.

He managed to negotiate a rental apartment in the Century on Central Park West (where he already had an office)—an unfinished space in the penthouse on the thirty-second floor that had originally been used by Jack Dempsey as his workout gym and then been renovated as an apartment by the Corning Glass family. It had views both over Central Park to the east and across the Hudson to the west, a balcony, three bedrooms, and three bathrooms (Dorchester boy from Boston makes good!)

A Yale architect friend of Eliot's completely renovated the space, giving us new windows, new structures, white walls, white leather furniture, and steel-and-marble tables. The old

Baldwin piano was hoisted up those thirty-two floors and refinished, and a collection of very old Imari porcelains stood out against the white bookshelves. It was antiseptic and minimalist, a study in expensively appointed spaciousness—and we probably both needed those astringent surroundings to keep our wildly fluctuating emotions as much in check as possible. We were estranged by the tragedy, but to save our marriage and Peter's ghosts and phantoms, we were willing to try again. When I moved in, I was depressed and ambivalent, and I never unpacked my boxes of books.

In time, the contradictions in our relationship finally became unbearable, and I had left Eliot for Englewood, New Jersey. We were both destroyed, estranged from each other, but still emotionally connected by tragedy, children, and friends.

By then, I was already flying regularly to Russia and back on precious-metals business, a lucrative occupation but an escape as well from the straightjacket we were trapped in.

This escape into Russia was for me, if not easy, certainly seductive; instead of feeling hemmed in and trapped by loss and betrayal, a glittering ambiance was calling out to me, and I surrendered gratefully to it.

Still, Eliot was always there to greet me at the airport when I returned from Russia.

But he had an address book filled with the names of married friends with silent, dissatisfied wives. Going through it much later, I wondered why peer professionals with families, what I thought of as our "normal friends," rarely appeared.

He spent a lot of his spare time in the West Side Y on Sixty-third Street, doing serious weight-lifting to get his body in order, and (I was told) regularly drifted into the biggest gay bars in town, where he met friends, art directors, architects, young Choate and Yale men, copywriters, actors—the list was endless. And he found time to drop by the Russian Bathhouse off First Avenue on Tenth Street, where it was warm and relaxed and dirty, and, on certain days of the week, men-only.

And then he was at the airport to greet me again. He wasn't looking well at all. No longer impeccably dressed, he was in gym clothes and complaining of flu and of another "viral infection." In total denial, I obsessively wondered why this healthy man was sick.

My daughter Lisa was in a medical residency program in

Boston then. She flew in to check on Eliot's illnesses. I met her in Eliot's apartment, and we had a long talk. Her mandate for the visit was, as she put it, to get "to the cause of the lesions causing the TIA."

Days later, she had him hospitalized in New York Hospital with full-blown AIDS and venereal diseases.

I drove myself to understand, not only what he was going through, but what had led him there—the thrill, the freedom, the power of being with other men and no holds barred, no limits. I thought long and hard as well about the varieties of self-loathing and deception that came with the thrill, and about the guilt he must have felt in intimate contact with stunning, muscular young men—lean and youthful and gorgeous—who often had no name, just an attractive face.

There was, however challenging it may have been for people as deeply in the closet as Eliot—a true gay paradise between Stonewall and AIDS. People came out in droves to friends and family, found ways to open up at work. The chain of relationships in which one might be *simultaneously* engaged, from a trick (an anonymous encounter), to a number (when the contact was memorable enough to exchange phone numbers), to an item (when you began to attract notice as a couple), to a boyfriend (in whose company you'd expect to be seen on Saturday night), to a lover (whom you always spent Sunday with), was breathtaking. It could be filled with jealousies, tests of fidelity, uncertainties, triumphs, and failures; but it was as real as sunlight. All that vanished in a matter of months as the tragic extent of the plague became clearer and clearer. Whole neighborhoods were decimated, and there was no way to stop it.

It's hard for people who weren't around then to imagine what AIDS looked like. It destroyed that complex world. It turned young men into old ones (those who survived at all). It made them ghosts, a plague that murdered beauty and promise. A young boy, my own secretary, wasn't feeling well, was sickly for a few weeks then on sick leave, and then I never saw him again; he had been murdered by AIDS in less time than it takes to get a dental implant.

And there was the stigma, the terror that swept through straight people who thought they could catch so lethal and (so it was thought) so contagious an illness, for which there was no cure or real treatment, as easily as a head cold—that it was airborne, or spread in saliva, or by touch. All of this was untrue.

Nor was it true that the plague was God's punishment of homosexual behavior, a rumor that turned the terror into a righteous frenzy even in the evolved liberal bastion of Manhattan.

All of it, for me and despite all the broken terrain between my husband and me, and how it fell hard upon Peter's death, had a greater, more monstrous impact on me even than the Holocaust and what I had gone through in those years. Decades after the Nazis, I was an adult with nuanced, adult sensibilities. But Dylan Thomas's stunning line, "After the first death, there is no other," is true, I think—and the terrors of a seven-year-old in a dark and silent world I have in some important ways never truly escaped from resonated in me, multiplied the sense of despair while Eliot struggled with the disease, and even more when he was gone. Now I keep photographs of him, with our kids and grandkids, on the mantelpiece above the fireplace. I've gotten over the horror of his suffering.

17
WALL STREET

█N THE SMALL PRECIOUS-METALS
world, my moniker "Zolotaya Susanna," earned from my
work in Mr. Filner's firm, had resounding cachet with firms
eager to introduce me to business with Russia's platinum-
group metals state agency. When I left to join AIG, international metals firms and big-shot officials coming to New
York wined and dined me, and one superb-looking wom-
anizer actually tried (without any luck) to seduce me. The
CEO of the one and only firm in New York representing
Japan, Sumitomo, listened attentively and said yes to all of my
proposed projects, smiling nonstop in an enthusiastically

condescending manner that made me suspect there was no horse in that corral. I followed up with him many times but could never reach the man, and never heard from his company again.

But Sumitomo was, blissfully, a rare exception. The buzz at the New York Mercantile Exchange was much more common—that Zolotaya Susanna's contacts and successes with Russia had made Mr. Filner rich. I had become something of a marvel for dealing with Russian businesses, particularly the state agency Almazjuvelirexport. Gary Davis, the CEO of the trading unit at AIG, wanted to discover what I was all about. He was impressed with my fluency in Russian, my graduate studies at Columbia University (his alma mater as well), and my resilience. I knew nothing about the long, lucrative history of AIG in China, but Davis clearly knew a lot about me. But I was very surprised that AIG, a firm with global clout, had no relationship at all with the autocratic precious-metals bureaucracy in Moscow.

Clearly, AIG and I had something to offer each other.

A week after I returned from my most recent Moscow trip with Filner, Davis telephoned to suggest that I pick a time to visit his office for conversation and an early morning meeting in the AIG offices on 70 Pine Street, where I could listen in and comment on the traders' daily strategizing before the market opened. He had heard of my recent successes with Noblemet's Filner and assumed that I would be what he called a "quick learn," ready for serious conversation. I said sure, and we confirmed a pickup.

In the lobby of the Century at seven in the morning, my Rolodex stowed in my monogrammed Tumi briefcase, I was ready. A limousine picked me up at exactly that time, and took me to Gary's offices. Looking back four decades later, I still marvel at my own courage that day.

It was my first time visiting Wall Street, a new world for me in New York. I was overwhelmed and astonished to see the combat zone, theater, and stage of bull-and-bear in action. The fact that AIG, a Fortune 500 behemoth, needed my help with Russia was even more surprising, since I hadn't as yet followed any of the dots to grasp that détente diplomacy and foreign policy had made Russia the new strategic frontier for commerce.

At 70 Pine, I took the elevator in the Art Deco AIG

building to the fourteenth floor. A secretary pointed to the room where traders gathered without telephones for discussion and analysis of activity in Asian and European markets. Traders also told of their successes from the previous twenty-four hours.

Sessions began promptly at eight. Davis supervised the best and the brightest Ivy League graduates, many reputedly the rebellious children of well-to-do professionals. Some recognized my face, surprised to see me there so early in the morning. The commodity market was about to open, and Gary and his troops were eager for battle.

I could sense the edgy, carnivorous energy of young traders returning to their desks. The area resembled a small section of a football stadium. In a wide horizontal space, traders sat elbow to elbow, forming a human chain. Between each chair and row there was not enough space for two people to pass each other without first turning sideways. They hunched toward computer screens, each juggling telephones, watching numbers flash by and murmuring with quiet concentration to secure orders from traders in Zurich, London, or Frankfurt before Europe closed.

As a child, I often felt a longing for affection from my father, a wish he had never satisfied. He'd always been present and absent at the same time. No hugging or kissing, or warm embraces. But at that moment, obsessing about my unrequited love from my father seemed far away and long ago. That yearning for love and protection, never fulfilled, was swiftly displaced by Gary Davis's appreciation of my smarts, good looks, and Russian connections. Always competitive, I knew he liked me, and I decided that AIG would be my big-time challenge.

American International Group is a multinational financial and insurance conglomerate with operations in more than eighty countries and jurisdictions. AIG companies employ 49,000 people. Its corporate headquarters are in New York City, with branches around the world, and it is one of the most prominent companies on the Fortune 500 list, with a current shareholder equity of $59 billion.

Hank Greenberg, the CEO and director of that empire when I joined the company, was also its largest stockholder. He presided over a vast and expanding empire. He consorted with, and lobbied for, the Communist regime in Beijing and was close with the mayor of Shanghai offices in a historic building on the Bund in Shanghai.

Greenberg's foreign policy influence reached very far. Long before Putin's meeting with U.S. President George W. Bush, Greenberg had met with Putin, then an obscure KGB operative, to discuss AIG's investments and methods for improving economic ties and relationships between the U.S. and Russia.

I followed Gary Davis around the trading room and back office accounting like a bulldog. I knew nothing about commodity exchanges, Nymex, Comex, open interest, supply and demand, or trader terminology. Intimidated and perplexed, I did ask Gary to explain a few financial terms: basis points, troy ounces, derivatives, and such. He glanced at me, and responded matter-of-factly, "You will learn quickly."

I was hired before lunch to begin the following Monday and was allowed to give three days' notice to Mr. Filner (the usual Wall Street M.O. was the same day). At AIG my salary and compensation package would double and also include round-trip car service from our penthouse on Central Park West to the building on Pine Street.

Davis had decided that I would share his office space (so

he could keep an eye on me). On my first day, he pointed me to an empty desk with telephones and a Quotron machine. On the desk I spotted a box of new business cards reading:

> AIG TRADING CORPORATION
> Susan Gold
> Director
> Commercial Department

Around lunchtime, pepperoni pizza and Diet Coke arrived at the desk of the commercial department of one, and Gary nonchalantly mentioned as well that Hank Greenberg would be stopping by for introductions.

Minutes later, the trading noise instantly subsided when Greenberg entered. Traders were uncomfortable, looking serious and working hard, as he wound his way around the room. Spotting me eating a slice of pizza, he stopped for a personal welcome.

He looked the part of a filled-out, retired marine. His eyebrows met at the bridge of his nose, and his keen, ruthless eyes could bore straight into you—his idea of intimacy. He waved his hand magisterially over the young people at their desks. "I don't understand what goes on inside their heads, so long as they create wealth for the firm." It was good theater for us. Sitting in Gary's chair, he leaned back, rested a shoe on an open desk drawer, and declared, "I've been studying the natural-resource market in Russia for a long time—tremendous opportunities, more promising than insurance in China. There's no Boxer Rebellion here! Russia is our next big market!" He pointed a finger at the ceiling. "And the most lucrative. We will open Russia, not only for investments, but for ideas about management, governance, and accounting standards." He had combined affable, disarming charm with a terrifying and intimidating management style for so long that the effect had become seamless. The staff compared it to being in the marines, that hierarchical sense of authority. He was a heavy hitter, fighting off threats and routinely outperforming competitors in far-flung domains. A pioneer of one of the biggest and most strategic global corporations, he took great pleasure from the aggressive, profit-driven culture that spawned commitment to innovation unlike that in any other company.

"With my counsel," he told me, "China has launched what

they call 'market socialism,' achieved rapid economic growth, and pulled hundreds of millions of peasants out of poverty. As they say, 'Getting rich is no crime'!"

He styled himself as the ultimate deal maker—there was lots of hubris about it to be sure, but it wasn't terribly far from the truth. "Soon I will be advising Boris Yeltsin as well," he said. "Russia needs *our* ideas and know-how."

Hammerin' Hank was swinging from the plate by then: "We'll be more productive there than Commodore Perry, who opened Japan long ago. Our Financial Products group is ultimately under my control. We must be the *first company on the block*—we have vast opportunities to outperform our competitors, to consolidate Russia ahead of our peers and capitalize on our investments." It was "Hooray for Our Team" talk in spades, as if he were running for president.

"We know that Russia is a black hole for investors," he went on. "But black holes offer opportunity. We will be working with a sovereign state. They need to modernize their asset base for commodities, and they have to raise financing on international markets. Our entrepreneurial history tells us there is no ownership of ideas," he said flatly. "Remember that.

Look beyond their books. Look outside the box!"

He wouldn't give up. His mind routinely flew from one possibility to the next, around and around Russia's vast natural resources and dollar signs. "Do you understand? Our collateral will be sovereign *Russia!*"

His goal in precious metals was to buy them cheaply, sell them to another investor dearly, and make money without taking any risk himself. By wagering large sums of money, creating a hedge, generating a demand for the metal, and selling it, he was convinced he'd succeed. The difference between what AIG paid for the metal and the "forward sale," or hedge, would represent the firm's profits on the deal, a standard trading procedure, with no exposure. It was a very simple strategy, and I learned it as if it were the eleventh commandment.

Listening to his missionary enthusiasm and anticipating my salary increase, I also realized that my interests were largely not at cross-purposes with Greenberg's business ethics.

He was ready to seize and dominate that part of the continent; that was his style. From the start, he sensed I had what it would take to help achieve this mandate. Overwhelmed and eager to work in Russia, I was to become the lynchpin between

Gary, Greenberg, and Russian natural resources, especially the platinum group metals.

Wishing me good luck, Greenberg left Gary's desk, and I took a deep breath.

My first project was to telex Moscow, formally indicating that, in the spirit of détente, I was "invited"—*priglashena*—as Commercial Director of AIG, a multinational company, to negotiate platinum group metals for American industries, a contradiction and oxymoron for capitalism and Marxist ideology!

I nervously studied my Rolodex, fishing out and telephoning old trading friends about my new position. I was still in training, happy but not ready for business. All of my contacts were impressed, respected my candor, and wished me luck as we chatted about geopolitics, central banks, and finance. Most *academic* colleagues, shocked and distrustful that I had what it took to make the leap to Wall Street, were resentful and jealous, eschewing all personal or political conversations.

After some weeks of listening, questioning, and paying attention to the young traders, Gary was ready for my department of one to "visit America," as he put it. I telephoned industrial consumers in San Francisco, Los Angeles, Houston, and Mexico City. I had learned from my Russian associates that personal attention (*vnymanie*) turned many wheels in our transactional world. In each city, I booked lunch at the best restaurant in town. Purchasing agents across America generally lead dull business lives, so they were happily impressed with my personal visit and fascinated with discussions about the Russian economy, politics, and first-hand cultural gossip. Never before had those men heard so much interesting personal and global information.

I returned to my Wall Street desk with future orders and requirement data from Corning, Amoco, and Chevron. With help from one of the in-house accountants, a lawyer, and Gary himself, I diligently structured customers' future industrial orders.

Once that was done, Gary decided that I was ready for my first AIG trip to Moscow—to plan for and establish our AIG office and infrastructure.

Two months later, buckled in as the Delta 747 I was flying rapidly dropped altitude, I was happy to see dirty, gas-streaked

Moscow beneath the wings. I was relieved as well to get out of the crowded but silent shuttle bus and set foot in the dingy airport, and I joined the long passport-arrivals line. Sheremetyevo Airport looked grim, shrouded in semi-darkness as if someone had forgotten to turn the light switches to full power. A young, beefy, very serious passport-control officer stared at me, glared at the visa and passport, checked them on a computer, grunted, and shoved the documents back at me without a word.

At last I entered Russia proper and headed to Baggage Claim to wait for my suitcases. Once I had them, I moved on slowly to Customs Control. All was in order until the customs officer searched my handbag and came across a valuable string of cultured pearls that I had neglected to declare on the customs form.

Delicately twirling the strand with two hands and coveting them, he summoned another official for protocol. "They are my wedding pearls—a gift from my husband!" I said flatly. "I want them back. I will call the American Embassy!"

Another twenty minutes went by with nothing still except quiet conversation, before a second customs official, one who took notes in a small book and insisted on speaking English, said, "No problem here. We give you document and hold item for safekeeping in internal affairs office safe, near Arrivals sign. You fill one more *anketa* ("questionnaire"), and pearls return when you fly out." I was frightened and tired from the flight and the hassles, and realized that my favorite necklace was gone, my sacrifice for setting foot in Mother Russia again.

I searched for a taxi to the city but couldn't find one that was not reserved. But I spotted an energetic young man waiting for the delayed domestic arrival of his uncle, a member of the lower *duma*. He was able to commandeer a baggage cart, and I followed him to his uncle's government-issued Zhiguli.

We got to town quickly, and I registered at the National Hotel, made famous by Lenin and the old Bolsheviks, and tipped the doorman with Marlboros. He bowed and almost curtsied, telling me, "Madame, *vy takye dobry*," (I knew very well that I was a generous customer!) as he opened the heavy oak door with a flourish.

I handed out lipsticks at the registration desk, and more lipstick and nylons to the concierge who would be noting my comings and goings, always with a big smile.

The following day, a legitimate taxi—and more Marl-boros—dropped me at the Radisson Slavyanskaya Hotel, an oasis in the center of Moscow, Russia's first deluxe Western-style hotel and business complex for foreign companies. I felt comfortable, as the rental office of the hotel was both welcom-ing and familiar. With help from a Dutch tenant, I was able to hire a chauffeur with a Lada; a personal secretary, Tanya; and a *computerchik*, Slava, who pragmatically resolved most tech-nical issues. I socialized with company representatives on the floor. The Brazilian office next door supplied coffee while a few of us grumbled about Moscow's bureaucratic indolence.

I made friends with the "flying Dutchman" (a represen-tative of KLM airlines) who personally drove me to see other fancy buildings where expatriates lived, and then finally to the residential building of the Hotel Ukraina. There I was lucky to rent an apartment—from a retired Bolshoi ballerina named Natalya who was ready to move into her parents' place—for $1,500.00 a month. The Ukraina is one of Stalin's seven gothic towers—old, gray, and craggy but super luxurious, built by German World War II prisoners.

She also followed me to the padded apartment door,

where she proceeded to drill me on the kinks and peculiarities of the five locks while sneering at the next-door neighbor, who had been waiting jealously to greet me and inquire about finding another expatriate tenant for her apartment.

I was nearly overwhelmed by shock and awe upon entering that double padded door! The apartment was appointed with lofty and ominous balcony windows, elegant plastered ceilings, and lustrous parquet floors. It had an eighteenth-century chandelier in the front hall, striking Karelian birch curves of the Biedermeier chairs in the main room, honey-colored woods, delicate inlayed marquetry, gilt mirrors, and many paintings by Russian avant-garde artists, including Natalia Goncharova and Mikhail Larionov. "I wanted to rent the apartment to a bachelor, an aesthete," she said as she showed me through the rooms. "My late husband was a collector and a diplomat. You must be a Bulgarian lady diplomat. You like my small art collection!"

"No, I am American, born in Ukraine—and I studied Russian in Columbia University."

"Ukraine! We are like sisters! I danced in Kiev long ago. Welcome to Moscow! Your professor must be Bulgarian. You speak with Bulgarian accent—not pure Moscow Russian but Bulgarian."

"Our company just opened an office in the Slavyanskaya for business," I replied. Natalya was uncomfortable asking about the nature of the business—no details, I figured, no evidence. As we chatted, she reached for her inscribed photo album of the Bolshoi Ballet, with pictures of the corps and a few personally inscribed principal dancers who had been her partners. She also showed me a rather elegant phonograph machine. "It works beautifully," she assured me, and turned up the volume on a lovely recording of Ippolitov's *Caucasian Sketches.* I closed my eyes and was on the verge of being swept away by the music when she leaned closer and whispered into my ear, "Remember, now—this house has always been listened to, and will always be." I nodded gratefully. There's a world of difference between knowing about something and *knowing* it.

I was excited about the apartment and impressed with her. We finalized our discussion with cash (which she stuck as a talisman inside her brassiere), cognac, and sweets. Discussing the logistics of the move was easy. With an informal (*poka*) at the door—"Yes, see you soon," I agreed—she blessed us as "soul mates" and handed me a small gift of a little compact mirror, with an artist's rendering of a nineteenth-century *devitsa*, a country maiden.

I knew, needless to say, that the dollar has always been king in Russia, and with access to hard currency, I was soon able to buy my own antiques privately and in *komissioniy* consignment shops, and Russian art, as well as the best tickets to cultural events.

Something under a year went by during which I patiently strengthened our business relationships all around. A slow, steady autumn rain had fallen over the city—gray stone, gray sky. Tanya, the secretary, gave me a look as I walked in. I responded by raising both hands to my temples, sat ramrod straight on the chair at my desk, sadness in my eyes, and watched people in the street below. I tried to force myself to go back to work but couldn't, so I continued looking at the *Moscow Times*.

The high point of my workday was the early evening conversation with New York. Slava was busy reading the Interfax news and studying a book, *Advanced Computer English for Dummies*, for the newly purchased computer. By six o'clock, as Tanya was preparing to leave, I waited for the telephone call from Mr. Greenberg. Still uneasy, I was staring at my phone, hoping to wrap up the day, when it rang.

"A telephone call from Mr. Greenberg," she announced. Feeling a sense of panic, half rising from my chair, I lifted the receiver.

"What's up, Susanna? What's happening in the Russian market, our new frontier?"

This was followed by a brief silence on the telephone, followed by an eruption of outrage: "Just some more bureaucratic flimflam! The old communists are only wearing new hats! Only lunch and dinner for the Russkies? No Bolshoi Ballet or opera? Another waste of time! . . . Look, Susanna, we don't know where we stand with the Central Bank! I'm ready to tell them all to go to hell."

"Yes, Mr. Greenberg. I am having lunch with Mr. Kulichkov this Wednesday to confirm dates of the remaining two shipments to KLM. Our first delivery from them was delivered as scheduled. I've only been in Moscow for less than a year. We have to keep our powder dry."

"The whole thing's a load of hocus-pocus," Greenberg declared. "We're the Mount Everest of multinationals, and you have to be the best and put AIG over the top, Susanna. Because if you're not, we'll find someone who will. Someone younger, Susanna, right? Someone with more drive and class, with more creativity, committed to innovation."

I was frightened and upset by such threats and intimidations from him. My personal feelings of insecurity (which, at this point in my story, have been laid out like a freshly filleted Dover sole) returned with a vengeance.

But there were very dark clouds forming on the horizon of our contractual agreement with the Russian Central Bank and Almazjuvelirexport, the Russian agency charged with executing the sale and delivery of the metal to our partners. The latter was a regular business dealing in diamonds and gold as well as precious metals; it had offices all over the world—including one in Greenwich, Connecticut, that had opened after the introduction of the catalytic converter to the automobile business.

In the United States, the Clean Air Act of 1970 had been passed. It mandated that all cars produced after model year

1975 be equipped with a "catalytic converter," a device designed by Engelhard Industries and Corning Glass that used
palladium to reduce harmful exhaust emissions. Later amend-
ments to this act in the 1990s had banned leaded gasoline sales
by 1995, amplifying the need for catalytic converters by automobile manufacturers and further increasing the demand for
palladium.

On the other side of the world, tougher emissions standards for automobiles were also being legislated in developed
countries, causing an unprecedented and completely unantic-
ipated spike in the global demand for palladium that was driving up the market price for the precious metal.

Greenberg was *aware* of these stricter regulations making
their way into law and the impact they would have on our business. But he could not readily translate that awareness into a
recognition of how destructive the blizzard of bad news could
be about Russian privatization of the precious-metals industry
as a declaration of sovereignty.

The first "tranche," or portion of the entire order of palladium specified in our contract, did get delivered, as agreed
to by the Russian Central Bank and Almaz. AIG had hedged

all three tranches to offset the investment and price risk for future delivery. The contract was watertight and foolproof, and dollars had been transferred for the sale of three tranches of palladium over all three delivery dates at the agreed-upon fixed prices.

The morning after my unnerving conversation with Greenberg, anxious and distressed, I telephoned one of my associates at Almaz to confirm the shipment of the next tranche of palladium. He responded in an official manner that differed markedly from our usual friendly conversations. "I cannot say," he told me. "There has been a chemical problem in Norilsk refinery. One smelter is not functioning." He knew that the price of palladium had spiked because of the catalytic converter legislation in the U.S.

I adopted his official tone to remind him, "The contracts were guaranteed by the Russian Central Bank and are legally binding. AIG and our partners have traded on that same price by hedging their positions in the futures market. This has been established protocol for commodities since the Great Depression. Comex and Nymex rules and regulations must be followed."

I wasn't about to let this one go, but I did my best to disguise my mounting anger. But my "friend," I quickly realized, was only being permitted to spin the official state narrative.

This narrative had been fashioned by the Kremlin's vertical hierarchy pressuring the Ministry of Nonferrous Metals and the Central Bank. It incorporated a mixture of nationalism, populism, and politics as ministries and the prime minister played their geopolitical chess game. Its essence was very clear: Russia's strategic assets in the Siberian permafrost must be controlled by Russia. All of its natural resources—from gold to nonferrous metals, diamonds, uranium, and minerals, as well as its vast fields of natural gas, were its *sovereign wealth*. Norilsk had been a source of power and profits, *but none of those profits stayed in Russia,* which had more gold than South Africa, and which could pump more oil than Saudi Arabia.

By 2000, Vladimir Putin had replaced Boris Yeltsin, and the *ad hoc* coterie of oligarchs that had been marketing its natural resources, with the much better organized and systematic kleptocracy that continues to exist in Russia—the nation officially nationalized all its natural-resource industries.

But in the absence of such an articulated state policy, all

the functionaries I dealt with could do was lie to me about the gravity of my situation. I met with Kulichkov of the Central Bank for dinner one night in a restaurant with silk wallpaper and glittering chandeliers. We chatted about this and that. I had two vodkas before I looked him in the eye and said, "What's going on?"

"Going on?" He shrugged. "Nothing at all. Nothing is going on, Susanna. You know how it is in Russia—everything takes time. It is as if we need to invent the wheel. You must of course be patient," he concluded, lifting his glass. "All will be well, I assure you." At that very moment, as if they had been wound up with a key like a clock or an automaton, white-gloved waiters appeared with our first course, and that ended the conversation.

Of course, our own people, trolling for press rumors and news about AIG and spikes in futures and derivatives, were either ignorant or lying just as enthusiastically to our own customers, who were desperate for their palladium, as the Russians were lying to us.

So in the end, all of my efforts—my trips to Wall Street, my meetings with Gary, AIG lawyers, and the financial officers to make progress on the proposed three-tranche palladium forward contract with Almaz—were inadequate and ended in catastrophe. The last two shipments were never made, and contracts be damned.

Not long thereafter, an unnamed AIG board member leaked a story to the *New York Times* that our firm was planning to fire a thousand people. For the first time, AIG was firing the smartest people, the best and the brightest for whom even yesterday did not exist, and the central code of behavior valued speed, risk, and cynicism over loyalty, responsibility, and commitment.

Finally sitting upright, strapped in at Sheremetyevo Airport, I watched Russia disappear as the plane lifted into the sky and clouds above. The dismal gray began to drop away.

The Delta 767 was mostly filled with business people going home after their own ventures and challenges in Russia. The attendant in business class approached with a tray of champagne flutes, and I raised one to myself, grateful that I was still alive, having survived that uncanny wasteland of murder and betrayal, too strong even for me. When the attendant came around again, I ordered a double Scotch to bring myself up to par.

Professional frequent fliers recognize each other by body language. I was sitting next to a drink-sodden expatriate, and when he began speaking, I realized that his voice was too high and needed to be brought down.

"Ah, hello!" I remarked. "We're both going home!"

"Yes, we are," he said glumly. "There are hundreds of us here in Moscow," he eventually added. "Some are hungry, and some rich and idle expatriates, trust-fund babies looking for adventure. I'm neither. Somewhere in the middle, I think—and this is my last run! I've had my fill of stunning blondes, all English teachers, beautiful bars, *blinis* with caviar, but it's impossible to get anything going for my *company*. This place has no future! It's a business catastrophe!"

"Join the club," I told him.

I encountered the usual culture shock at JFK, but I was happy to be home. And again came a dry run about my feelings of self-worth, my sense of kudos in AIG's master gamble for vast fortunes, and my huge personal fiasco.

By the time I made it back to the southern tip of Manhattan, I understood very clearly that our conglomerate had fallen on hard times. The firm was going through the most concentrated turmoil in its history. The futures market panic that reverberated through the financial markets, and Russia's politics, had catapulted our trading group at AIG into a deep crisis. The world of money was in upheaval. Hundreds of millions of dollars had been lost in commodities.

This news was not completely unexpected since, while still in Moscow, I'd heard from our London office that the AIG board of directors was asking for a prompt meeting to review our Russian business.

I was jet-lagged and ill at ease back in Gary's office. An internal memo flashed across the Quotron machines: Failure of Russian palladium deliveries and events outside AIG's control have forced management to take quick action, cut back on staff, and prune intelligently.

Wall Street had turned on its own "band of brothers." I realized, it need hardly be added, that I was a commodity myself and could be canned and sold like tomatoes. Senior management took the path of least resistance and fired the most recent additions to the office—a massacre of innocents, young people easy to sack. They had not yet built connections within the firm and had no voice. Once fired, they immediately lost the right to remain on the trading floor. A security guard would take their passes. Their arrogance and self-confidence got stripped too in the process, and they emerged shell-shocked. A few, when asked for their passes, shouted at security guard to "fuck off" and returned to the trading floor for a good deal of weeping and hugging. It was an unusual scene: No one *ever* cried on the trading room floor or showed the least trace of vulnerability or need for human kindness. In a rapid reign of terror, traders were banished from the building, escorted to the elevator dragging personal belongings, gym clothes, sneakers, and extra shoes.

The next day, a welcoming message came from Greenberg, inviting me for tea and a debriefing. Since Guilt is my middle name, I faulted myself for the palladium disaster. Panicky and demoralized, I anticipated the worst.

18
THE TWENTIETH FLOOR

A COMPLETE HUSH SURROUNDED Greenberg's suite on the twentieth floor of 70 Pine Street, a city landmark and a historic art deco skyscraper, that day. His offices suggested both imperial and low-profile executive power. From this aerie, he ruled over one of the world's largest companies like a regent. He had worked ceaselessly for thirty-five years to build the top multinational firm in the country.

He spent his days amid majestic splendor, the complete opposite of the floors below, which were crowded with entrepreneurial chaos, a rough-and-tumble center of commercial buzz, money-making, and risk-taking—like a casino without the alcohol. I had been happy in Moscow, relieved that I didn't have to wake up every morning to the prospect of Hank Greenberg ready to bite the ass off every bear on Wall Street. He had what it took—hadn't he been decorated with a Bronze Star for meritorious service storming the beach at Normandy?

Once I made it past the receptionist and the pool of secretaries, an Asian butler—straight as a broom and clad in a white jacket—invited me into the reception room, and then, in time, through another door into the inner sanctum where streaming, dappled light came through the heavy open drapes. It was another world. Elegant Persian carpets further enhanced a strange, almost primordial silence. Exquisite antique grass cloth-papered walls were adorned with a large sepia photograph of the Normandy invasion, signed photographs of U.S. presidents from Eisenhower to Clinton, and a photo portrait of his glamorous trophy wife hugging two Maltese terriers. Chinese vases bookending his desk looked like imperial

Chien-lung (one dared not look for the reign marks), and a bonsai tree, garden, and waterfall offered nostalgic echoes of the company's insurance-business origins in China.

Glancing out the curved windows, I saw sweeping, panoramic views of the city, with tiny cars and people scurrying below in every direction.

I was still standing when Greenberg rose to greet me, shifting to a comfortable chair opposite mine.

"Welcome! Interesting issues in Moscow, I understand. Tell me about them." He invariably began with such an inquiry, a throwback perhaps to his training with the marines.

Finding my tongue again, I replied, "To contradict the Russian expression, all is not *normal'no*. Russia is Zaire with permafrost." I walked him through our palladium disaster, the opaque and Byzantine business environment, the sordid connections between organized crime and the State, the corrupt bureaucrats who had become entrepreneurs at the mercy of oligarchs and their own higher-ups.

Greenberg listened carefully, remained gracious, and said nothing. Increasingly ill at ease, I went pale and stared at the decorations of the Chinese vases.

Soon, he quietly asked, "And what did you learn?" returning to a statesmanlike calm, a mood more deliberate than
evangelical. The butler returned with tea service. My knees
were shaking; I was barely able to keep the cup from spilling
and could not speak.

"I've watched you closely since you joined us," he said into
the silence. "I've been following your career. You may not
have realized it, but I've taken a special interest in your development, and we have been satisfied with your challenging
work." He continued his diplomatic waltz. "You acted very
honorably. You were under tremendous duress, especially after
the loss of a child. We're grateful for what you did for us, and
we're aware of the cost to you, professionally and personally.
You've done a good job for the company. You've performed a
valuable service. . . . But even the little you know is too much.
We can't let you wander around Russia and Europe with our
intellectual property in your head. Much too dangerous, and
too much liability for you and the firm." His expression was
glacial, his voice terse and effective. "If you honor your non-
disclosure agreement, that should provide a full measure of
compensation. On our terms, naturally. . .but the sum would

be large."

It could have been worse. I was being forced to resign before I had the opportunity to quit, and float down the short distance to Earth. My severance was indeed generous, based on tenure. I could barely manage the closest thing to a smile when Hank reached out to shake my hand. My passion was spent. There is no redemptive value in suffering. Nothing happens by chance.

There was a sharp scent of autumn on the serene and misty afternoon I returned to New Jersey. I was exhausted but exhilarated and grateful to be home, ready to hang up my traveling boots and settle for a less arduous life of writing and an adjunct professorship at SIPA—the School for International Affairs at Columbia. It was almost the peak of the season, leaves at their most beautiful: gold, deep russet, orange to pale lemon yellow, a riot of color on the hillside nearby, a kaleidoscope you never see in Russia.

19
DAVID IN VERMONT

IT SOUNDS LIKE A FANCY PLACE. One imagines a comfy village in the English Midlands in, say, 1840, where people spend their days producing silverware and presentation pieces, and where respectful journeymen whip off their caps in the presence of their betters, those robust entrepreneurs who Made England Great.

That's not what Sheffield, *Vermont*, is about. It's a dirt-poor village—population, some seven hundred—chiefly composed of farmers and working people, and their families. There's a white clapboard church, a city hall, and a tiny post office open only two hours each morning where neighbors stop for mail and chat about the weather, politics, recent local events, and the economy.

Sheffield is also an almost all-White town in one of the Whitest states in America; recent statistics confirm that around three percent of its inhabitants are persons of color. There are historical reasons for that percentage: Vermont never had a large slave population because it was made up of small farms and other holdings rather than plantations and factories, and, politics aside, didn't need slaves to work the fields; as a result, it has been dominated by Anglo-Saxon people since its founding.

During periods like the Great Migration after Reconstruction failed in the South, no established force drew African Americans to Vermont either—lacking family or friends in the state, or job openings in large factories, African Americans went to the larger Northern cities like New York and Chicago, where they could find both.

Vermont's continuing Whiteness presents more of a puzzle until you realize that an outsider's most cherished images of the state—snow-covered country dotted with red barns, maple-syrup production, hunters in denim mackinaws—are all coded very White. It was, to be sure, the first state in the Union to abolish slavery, leans far to the left politically, and was the first to recognize same-sex couples. But it's *still* hard to find work there, and the locals (true New Englanders to the core) tend to keep their distance from outsiders. Racial bias against Blacks, I want to make clear, was hardly if ever an issue for us. Vermonters express their racist feelings against *red* people, Native Americans, more than against blacks like Veva, David Zimmerman's wife, and their two sons, Jacob and Tobias.

I discovered Sheffield because of David. Finally, in my seventies, I had been lucky enough to reclaim life with a partner and friend. He spun my disheveled life and broken dreams into empathy and love for others. The story of my journey with him is the story of everyone who has somehow lost their way and must find one back to themselves.

We first found each other at Brandeis University in 1952 but reconnected half a century later, at a class reunion. We were quite accidentally sitting at the same table. He was from the Midwest and had transferred to Brandeis from the University of Chicago. I'd thought him good-looking and interesting. Alas, as an intellectual rebel, a writer, and the editor of the college newspaper, he had not satisfied my mother's mandate that I marry a doctor.

At the reunion, I barely recognized David. He was withdrawn and sad. The sparkling, mischievous eyes were not there, nor was his old sense of humor. Our alumni friends were genial, laughing and drinking as they recounted stories of life and early college adventures, but David did not participate. Mostly, he stood apart from the crowd, a voyeur, speaking only to people who recognized and greeted him first.

Ignoring the solitude of my life, I was sociable and friendly and full of projects and activities, quietly marketing *The Eyes Are The Same* while I observed him.

I'd been told that he and his wife Veva had escaped New York City and retired to a homestead in rural Vermont. He was grieving for her; she had passed away after a long struggle with cancer.

At breakfast the next morning, I was eager to have him sit beside me. I was at once both surprised and not surprised by this eagerness. The distance that stretched between us was at once infinite and nonexistent. Fifty years later, with more insight into the nature of things than we'd had as college kids, we had a lot to say to one another, reminiscing about families, professions, and life in general.

My family had skied the mountains of Vermont many years earlier, and I had always been curious to see what Vermont looked like without snow. I told David as much. He extended an invitation to come and see, and I enthusiastically accepted.

When I got there, a different world lay close at hand. I was overwhelmed by the mountains, foothills, and valleys, the extraordinary open sky, the pageant of luminescent clouds, the trees a kaleidoscope of brilliant autumn colors, open vistas.

Decades fell away. The early autumn sun turned things to gold. The pungent smell of manure in the fields, roosters crowing, and cows mooing were nearly a constant. I was soon falling in love with Nature all over again, at one once more with the kid on a bicycle I had been, feeling the wind in her hair.

The following summer, I moved in with David, and spent many summers in the Northeast Kingdom. It's where my relationship with myself changed.

I found peace and serenity. It's still hard to believe, but I did. We tramped through the woods surrounding the village, and every step, every glance, had a new meaning—the reflection of a world transfigured by the awareness of truly loving and being loved. I listened for the laughter of children at recess in the local school, which bordered our property.

Our evenings at home were filled by a sense of peace and silence, a fleeting paradise that lived on without a need for conflict. We had a sense of communion in that solitude, were happy with being together, and negotiated time so we were certain that every moment was the essence of what life should have offered but that we had never before received or reached for. We were living as children do, cherishing the moment, unburdened by awareness of life's finitude.

A love affair no longer claimed the uniqueness of a grand passion. After suffering and growing old, we found new ways of loving one another. As tortured beings with pains already internalized, our attachment had broken free from the world with its absurdities, its lies, and its ugliness. We came there to live and enjoyed it for years.

Yards were ablaze with irises, poppies, and other spring flowers. Bright-blue morning glories clambered up the iron posts and along the steps.

David fished for brook trout across the road, in a stream that was protected by a huge old beaver who disliked it when David swam in it. We watched birds that came to the feeders and returned me to my Ukrainian childhood. The town where I was born had been a beautiful and remarkable place to live, and, it had seemed almost at once—the interval was so brief—as cruel as any place on the face of the Earth. But I knew from the moment David took me to Vermont that, however long it might take for the locals to strike up a conversation with me, I would never have to fear the sudden pounding of hobnail boots in our house.

Higher on the ridge, the hardwoods were just budding out. Crimson flowerets fallen from the sugar maples lay strewn near the brook. Painted trillium, with raspberry-stained throats, were still in bloom. Warblers—green, blue, black, yellow—lashed through the treetops. The woods rang with their mating calls. I heard songbirds and saw wildflowers and more. Once, we came upon a full-grown moose. The animal, which seemed to be in the final stages of distemper, had evidently staggered onto our property. The backyard apple trees were dropping their pink and white petals. Peas and lettuce were flourishing. The north wind out of Canada, known locally as the Arctic Express, had brought Sheffield its usual late spring blizzard, later than usual, burying the young peas in some gardens and the yellow-and-blue pansies.

Black fly time came after that.

Roadside ditches were pink and purple with wild lupines. High on the ridge, the new leaves of the hardwoods were still more yellow than green, and the sunlight fell through the foliage in a rich golden haze. Drifting down the trail above my head came a progression of brilliant yellow-and-black swallowtail butterflies. In the shrouded and dense Vermont woods, you can find the mysteries and sorrows of mankind.

The color of the late summer sky was mesmerizing, as were the dazzling white homes of the mill workers in the twilight; splashes of scarlet and gold appeared overnight and were set off handsomely by the dark green spruces and firs. Late-blooming phlox, hot pink and deep red, and a dozen multicolored daylilies all recently replanted, grew around the house. Beyond the shack, the brook murmured.

In the fall of the year, the Northeast Kingdom of Vermont is the most beautiful place on the face of the Earth, so beautiful that, if you go there alone, it hurts your heart not to have someone to share it with. Along the river east of the village, fewer than half a dozen barn lights now glimmered through the mists. A few chalets, second homes of city people, had gone up here and there in the woods. A ski resort was being planned on Burke Mountain. A four-lane superhighway from Boston was snaking its way up from Southern Vermont. The road grew steeper and narrower as I entered the woods and was covered with fallen leaves. The woods smelled ripe with decay and were bright with the red leaves of soft maples, toast-colored beech, golden yellow birch, purple ash, and the polished yellow leaves of sugar maples. Bright hardwoods began to give way to firs and spruces.

Beyond, to the west of the Green Mountains, a village ran due north and south in a long, jagged line. To the east, the peaks of the northern White Mountains gleamed with early

September snow. And then the Kingdom spread out before me in all its autumn enchantment. From there, you could look north into Canada.

The room I spent so much time writing in smelled like old oiled wooden floors, like furniture polish and officialdom. Although it was only mid-August, there was a dusting of snow on Jay Peak. A few leaves on the village elms had already turned yellow, and some of the swamp maples along the river had begun to redden.

Outside, as dusk fell, I often pointed out the window toward the afterglow of the sunset behind the mountains. A run of warm days and cool mountain nights held all week. Framed by abrupt green hills rising to darker green mountains. A sunny afternoon seemed utterly free of strife and care, like a Currier and Ives lithograph (yet another ingrained image that screams White).

But when that sun slid behind a bank of clouds and the scene of the painting faded from mid-to-late afternoon, I could see another Vermont. The elms on the street were not only leafless but dead. The green was sere and brown as though no rain had fallen in many weeks. The village houses were dingy and peeling. Not a sign of life appeared anywhere.

The countryside beyond the village seemed abandoned as well. Farmhouses and barns had collapsed into the overgrown fields around them. Once-cleared pastures had been overrun by redtop grass, barberry, juniper, and thorn apples—and I realized that I was looking at yet another eradication of a way of life. The tableau of the village never did regain its old and vivid summer colors. It continued to fade into a somber reminder of its original splendor—a faded image. The railroad and the mill have both shut down. Houses have fallen into disrepair. The farms in the surrounding hills have continued to go under until, today, there are only a handful left. Those have barely survived in the grip of tight regulations, falling prices, and a poor economy. They can only make a profit on the hay they sell. Raw milk and meat are too heavily regulated to sell without legal repercussions. Driving down the street, we see many empty houses and barns falling apart.

The population is dwindling now, too; the well-educated and progressive residents escape to brighter pastures while the less-educated locals remain. The opiate epidemic and crime have badly hurt the town as well. The ethic of work and self-reliance has all but disappeared. Transparent poverty is abundant.

Yet despite high unemployment rates, many people don't want to work. The welfare system is manipulated very well by the poor, and residents receive support for housing foster children and caring for children with special needs, and benefit from the checks from Social Security or Disability.

The extent of these supports reminded me of the Russian socialist system, under which the government supplied all forms of social welfare including housing, food, and utility assistance, and free education, healthcare, childcare, and medicine. Citizens in Russia; Russian immigrants in Brighton Beach, Brooklyn; and people in Sheffield, Vermont, are experts at gaming the system to receive maximum government aid while stealing from the state.

There are also plenty of tattoos in town, and plenty of motorcycles and firearms—shotguns, rifles, handguns, you name it. There's theft as well, and a belief in psychics, astrology, the presence of spiritual energy in inanimate objects like mountains and trees, and reincarnation. Currier and Ives are long gone.

But Vermont remains a retrospective place; the village evokes rest, repose of age, and devotion to the past, to memories. The Nabokov of *Speak, Memory!* would have found much to enjoy in this repose. I can certainly reconstruct *my* early Ukrainian childhood half a world away. In my mind's eye, I revert to my childhood home: I see sepia photographs of early village life in Western Ukraine, and with them a sense of sound and smell of a long-repressed, distant past, of horses and cows, sheep, pigs, chickens, roosters, and the pungent smell of manure in the fields. I see men swishing scythes and sickles, building mountains of hay at harvest-time, when I was allowed to have special adventures of hide-and-seek, sinking into scratchy grasses among the inverted cones; I see the house, the orchards, the fields of potatoes and wheat, the wildflowers, lumberyards, and meadows, something like a child would draw.

I don't like large-scale things. Something small and self-contained remains a moral and aesthetic ideal for me. Nostalgia for a better age that's gone simply heightens the awareness we have managed to engineer this century.

The local grocery store closed one year, and the next bottle of milk and newspaper were suddenly seven miles away. In W.H. Auden's Eden, all news was disseminated through gossip; he might have loved Sheffield too for that, because the gossip there is constant and omnivorous—if you don't know what you're doing, your neighbors do.

In Sheffield, the sounds of cows and chickens, the neighing of horses, the smell of manure on the fields, even the crow of a rooster in the morning, call up hay harvests—men building those mountains of hay, and me playing hide-and-seek among the ricks that were so much a part of my early youth. Now, small purring tractors tow rotating blades and heavy machinery to cut, spin, and organize the grasses into bales for easy transport and storage. Yet decades fall away to multicolored meadows with islands of yellow buttercups and mustard, purple lichen and vetch, and blue cornflowers, all reaching upward to the northern light warming the timber everywhere it touched. The late summer, the early autumn air, the golden light of the afternoon, strangely reminded me as well of the cold winter in a bunker under a barn very long ago, cold and always frightened on my thin straw mattress, sleeping on a pillow full of dried peas.

Except for my college years and two smart, sensitive, and wonderful children, my life has been a continuous crossing of mine fields—first as a "hidden child" surviving the Holocaust, then facing a difficult and traumatic marriage, followed by the loss of my youngest son and, later, the loss of a good and secure relationship with Eliot. Through all of it, I soldiered on.

Grit and determination drove me as well to survive in the professional world. Fluent in languages, at ease with history and international relations, I became a careerist and later a high-level executive in a multinational firm. When I retired, I began teaching and writing. At the Brandeis reunion, as I have said, I could as a result be sociable and interesting as I subtly marketed my book of memoirs and, even more significantly, was conscious and able enough to pay attention to David, standing away from the crowd.

Perhaps in compensation for all that energy, drive, and refusal to be stymied by the implacable forces of life (to paraphrase Hemingway, people can be destroyed but not defeated), I have become a creature who spies on her own life, a shamelessly self-involved sentimentalist, since even the most skeptical and fearful must permit themselves to indulge in certain illusions. A damaged and complicated past is a valuable commodity in today's literary market. I have tacitly managed to come to terms with the misfortunes that befell five-year-old me and that I have, I think, amply described here as well as in my earlier memoir—how, ineluctably and inevitably, those years left me unable to be certain of anything apart from myself, persuaded me that I had to rely entirely on myself, and burdened me with profound survivor's guilt for my brother and all the other children.

My computer illiteracy, and the rapid, inexorable pace of our digital revolution, have made it difficult for me to write at all—drafts of chapters have piled up like drifts of sand under the prevailing winds of my subject, to say nothing of the pace of everyday living. But I have said, I think, what I needed to in this book.

20
RUSSIA

WINSTON CHURCHILL DESCRIBED Russia as "a riddle wrapped in a mystery inside an enigma." F. Tyutchev, a classic nineteenth-century poet, believed that understanding Russia is a leap of faith: One can only "believe" in Russia, and trust in Russian exceptionalism.

Recently in New York, I met a Russian artist who tried to explain why his compatriots are so despondent when they get to America. Like most self-respecting Russian artists who end up emigrating, he was a pretty active dissident. And yet, he told me, his eyes filling with a revealing fire, he felt convinced that Russia was the greatest—really, the only—country in the world. "We defeated the Germans in the war, we had the greatest literature in the world, we had the greatest culture. It was such a pride," he said intently. I looked back, trying to understand. National pride? It seems, for our globe, a terribly old-fashioned sentiment. I hardly know what it means now in the United States.

In another conversation, a United Nations Russian correspondent expressed a different sentiment: "You can never understand us because Russia still doesn't understand itself."

Similar insights have been expressed by Russians, both young and old, workers and intellectuals, across all political spectrums, for centuries.

The intelligentsia have struggled for two centuries to determine whether or not it is morally tolerable to write in an autocracy without attempting to end the autocracy, which has dominated life in Russia seemingly forever, since well before the Eastern Orthodox Church and Byzantium.

The people ("*narod*") and Bolsheviks organized coups,

demonstrations, strikes and revolutions, gulags, and genocides. *Plus ça change, plus c'est la même chose.*

Historians are forever peeling that onion (or opening the *matryoshka*). Russia is broader and more diverse, stranger and more contradictory, than any idea of it. It resists all theories about what makes it tick, confounds all the paths to its possible transformation. Sprawled across eleven time zones, it encompasses most of Eastern Europe and Northern Asia, has the world's largest total land mass—a sixth of the world total— and is 6,000 miles from St. Petersburg to Vladivostok, 2,500 North to South; it possesses vast oil reserves, gas, and mineral resources—including nickel, gold, diamonds, cobalt, and platinum group metals, as well as $600 billion in foreign reserves. Russia's population now stands at 160,000,000, with many regularly leaving when they can.

Putin's geopolitics today simply continue Russian terror and autocracy—grievances, paranoia, and an imperialist mindset have always been part of Russian life. The longer the Ukrainian war lasts, the more Russian society is cleansing itself of liberalism and "Western poison"—Putin, the church, and the ultraconservative right have dragged the system back to

the brutal and archaic public stance it has exercised throughout almost all of its previous incarnations. Civilians and children have been uprooted and killed. Cities and villages in
Ukraine have been destroyed. The Russian offensive has tar-
geted civilians, hospitals, and all manner of public institutions,
aiming to obliterate, not an opposing army, but an entire re-
sistant population.

Ukrainian and Russian soldiers have perished in this
genocide. Western Europe has qualitatively changed. The
world order is threatened, while hundreds of thousands of
refugees have fled to the Czech Republic, Germany, Poland,
Moldova, Finland, and some to Israel and America.

The greatest freedom resulting from the Soviet collapse,
the freedom to travel or leave the country, is no longer possible. After seven decades of Soviet socialism, Putin's current
road leads nowhere.

All my life, in different ways, I have enjoyed and loved
Russian culture. It began, I think, with those songs and
fairytales I first heard from my Russian-speaking nanny—the
only time my father trumped my mother's household directive.

He insisted that we hire Olga, who had spent several eventful years living in Russia. It was she who first introduced me to Petrushka, a puppet who, cursed with a human heart, sad and alone, locked in a dark room, silently cried out his despairing love for an unfeeling ballerina who had spurned him and caused his destruction.

In the Russian fairytale books Olga brought for me, I met a prince in turned-up boots who rode through the Russian forest, talked to animals, and braved the strongholds of the cunning witch Baba Yaga and the evil sorcerer Kacheri the Immortal.

In the darkness of those deep forests, the Hunchbacked Horse was ready to carry the brave-hearted to their life's desire, the gray wolf became a friend, and the Firebird's feathers gleamed. As a child, I devoured these stories, which seemed more alive to me than my own life.

Over the years I found joy and inspiration in Russian poetry, prose, art, architecture, music, and dance—and even the sound of the language. I've studied the history, learned the language, and spent much time working in the country. Led by the feathers of the Firebird, beyond the stories of cruelty, beyond the gray monotony of the land of today, I have always found beauty.

Through the years, I've met many people who share my admiration for the artistic traditions and culture of this great land fragmented by the blows of history. Yet the artistic achievements of Russia are often viewed as isolated phenomena and not as vital offshoots of a society that had achieved much and, had it not been destroyed, could have achieved much more.

For an assortment of reasons, some understandable and others difficult to grasp, it is the darker side of Russia's history that has most often been emphasized—not only in the Soviet Union and whatever it is that replaced it, but also in the West. As a result of this lopsided focus, the picture of old Russia (every nation has an older version of itself) as a fabric of many textures, characterized by a full measure of grace and beauty, is not presented. I have therefore concentrated here on describing that beauty that the Russians know so well how to create, what they love and admire, and how they live.

The Russians know the darker side of humanity, but they also understand the extraordinary capacity of the human soul for sacrifice and love, and they have the ability to accept both sides of man with greater equanimity than we in the West. They know how to take a long view as well—something we have all but forgotten in our frenzied desire for immediate gratification.

Here's one glimpse into the profound differences between our cultures: In Russian, the words "frustration" and "sophistication" do not exist. Historically, the Russians have valued humility rather than pride. They have approached God in a spirit of meekness. They have loved nature. They have revered poets and poetry with a passion equaled by few other peoples and have produced a poetic literature of extraordinary richness and variety. Their knowledge of suffering, and their understanding of human weakness, have made their nineteenth-century novels probably the greatest in world literature. Russians have transformed ballet from an amusing entertainment for the nobility into a serious art form for a discerning public.

In July 1944, when we were liberated by Russian soldiers marching west to take Berlin, I remember my father's smile when he first crept up the barn ladder to speak with the young soldiers. His first question was about his long-lost rebel relative, Semyon Geller, a distant cousin.

But why care about a single drop in the bucket of Russian history? At a time when our eyes are exhausted by the Ukrainian dead and the uprooting of a peaceable way of life we see in full color on TV and in magazines and newspapers, how can one young man's acts on behalf of his beliefs in a distant time matter? It was important for my father.

Semyon was a journalist and editor of the weekly gazette in Włodzimierz. In the early 1930s, while he was still working there, he announced that he had become a Communist Party member and a Bolshevik, and that he was leaving to become a political activist in Moscow. "Our Bolshevik revolution had raised its flag [there]," he wrote, "and we proclaim the link between Russia and the fate of the whole world."

Months later, still before the Nazi occupation, the family received a telegram from Semyon. He was settled and working in Moscow for the party newspaper *Izvestya*, a tightly controlled publication for the Communist empire whose chief editors were part of the Soviet leadership. In fact, the newspaper provided the official Communist narrative and practically served as a set-bible of life instructions for the party elite.

Working with AIG, I frequently spoke to my parents and children in the States. Each time I did, my father asked if I had been able to discover anything about Semyon, pleading with me to help discover his fate: "After all," he said, "family is family."

I became curious as well and scheduled a visit to *Izvestya*. Two assistant editors confirmed Semyon's work there but were unable to provide more information. They had no address for him but suggested that, if he was still alive, he must be retired, a "pensioner," and that I might find his address in the Moscow archives.

Once I was permanently settled in Moscow and had lots of free time after lunches and concerts to lobby for our palladium financial services contract, I challenged myself to investigate my lost relative further. I delegated the initial telephone inquiries to my assistant Tanya. Sadly, she discovered, all the telephone numbers for the state archives were either obsolete or wrong.

Finally, someone somewhere advised her that some 430

Moscow archives and manuscript repositories had been moved to a new location, a quaint Moscow street—Ulitsa Vyborgskaya—in the Voykovsky District.

We promptly wrote a letter on official AIG stationary to the Department of History and Records, Ministry of Foreign Affairs, Russian Federation, requesting permission to begin research on Semyon Geller, a reporter for *Izvestya*.

As instructed, I enclosed a Sberbank (official government bank) check for $80.00 and a photocopy of my passport, hoping for a reply.

Surprisingly, the response was prompt—but the search was endless, frustrating, and maddening. The Russian State Archive of Socio-Political History (RGASPI) is a large Russian state archive, based in Moscow, which contains pre-1952 archives of the Communist Party of the Soviet Union (CPSU). It is managed by Rosarkhiv, established in 1999. This archive also manages the Russian Centre for the Preservation and Study of Documents from 1954 to the present.

Renovated by Turkish workers, it's a three-story 1920s townhouse clad in yellow-beige stone, with wide windows in front, and an aspen and a poplar tree rising in front of it to the height of the building, shadowing the middle of the street.

I obsessively spent many afternoons there sitting in a stiff and uncomfortable high-back chair under direct, bright lighting. Aside from archives of the Russian Federation, it contained documents from many other sources, including personal repositories, and records of Soviet Russia as an independent state (1917–1922) and as a territorial entity of the USSR (1923–1991).

I soon realized that its 430 archives and updated manuscript repositories are linked to, and controlled by, the Ministry of Foreign Affairs, the Foreign Intelligence Service, and Russia's Permanent Mission to the United Nations. Clear-eyed and sober, I managed to process my denial and connect the dots about my experiences in real time instead of the Russian fairytales of my nanny.

One day after work I shared my frustrations about these archives with a business neighbor, the Russian KLM assistant. She mentioned that her aunt, Olga Andreevna, a graduate of Moscow University, was a chief librarian at the State Archives.

Olga turned out to be a pioneer and super-professional in the practice of librarianship. Maintaining these archives was sacred work for her, and she could help me in my search, especially since my neighbor was the aunt's favorite niece. We arranged for introductions the next day.

Discovering and working with Olga was like discovering America! I assured her that I was not an evil capitalist but a lover of art and books doing geographical research for a multinational company, and a business neighbor of Katya, her niece; and I gifted her with a festive box of Belgian chocolates from the hard currency store. History shapes strange reciprocities by providence or chance. That is one of the odd pleasures of thinking about history, including one's own, whether one believes it to be moved by chance, or providence, or the secret cunning of the dialectic.

Olga listened attentively and understood my queries, excused herself, and promised to return soon. An hour or so later, she appeared pushing a lopsided old wooden dolly that contained Semyon Geller's magic box—-a carton containing his life and destiny.

Pasted directly on top of the box was an official copy of Khrushchev's famous 1953 speech to the Politburo exposing Stalin's crimes and the rehabilitation of Russia's prisoners as "traitors to the motherland." Under Stalin, the press had only one clear purpose: during War Communism, it was a tool for the demonization and denunciation of the "enemies of the state." It still is today.

Other personal items included Semyon's passport information, a Moscow address, an identification card from the Russian Association of Proletarian Writers, and one identifying him as the official journalist for Kinofilm. He had indeed been hired as a reporter for *Izvestya*. He wrote propaganda stories, "agitprop," about the Bolsheviks' first Five-Year Plan, about the *udarniki*—educated people who volunteered and sacrificed hard labor in new industrial regions to satisfy the urgent needs of agricultural collectivization.

"For generations," he wrote, "the *kulaks* have farmed the land for themselves, organizing the local peasant labor to their own ends. But the time has come for 'common land must serve the common good.'"

At the peak of the terror caused by Stalin's repression, Semyon Geller was summarily arrested and convicted. No more of his stories appeared in *Izvestya* after 1950. The very same newspaper accused him, stating that his defense of *kulaks* was merely a refuge for groups of the counter-revolutionary intelligentsia.

I found other legal papers rife with lies and sinister accusations and directives in those archives: his appearance before the People's Emergency Committee of the People's Commissariat for Internal Affairs; an addendum to the expansion of the Criminal Code to allow the arrest of anyone expressing dissension; a document charging him with criticism of *kulak* collectivization, as referenced in the criminal code for corrective labor 192K-1.

Finally, I came upon a document from a deputy officer of the *gulag* camp in Belomorkanal, where he perished as a *zek*, a political prisoner.

So yes, history is sly, and shapes strange reciprocities. As a Holocaust survivor, my goal in the study of history has always been how I explain, come to terms with, understand, and trace my personal narrative of the war and the Holocaust when I lost my childhood.

And there in that mellow-looking townhouse on a quiet street in Moscow, I had discovered a distant relative, a victim himself who became a friend and allowed me to follow the dots of his remarkable moral journey and personal struggle to survive.

Digging down further with Olga, we found an old and faded leather address book. Touching the crumpled leather, we quietly read notes, addresses and annotations, passport information, and his Moscow address. I felt I was speaking intimately with Semyon himself.

After some time, I was able to decipher jottings and remarks of grim notes on every page: "Exiled. . . . Disappeared . . . . Dead. . . . Killed in battle. . . . Shot by the enemy. . . . Shot by his own side." I ran my fingers over the tattered leather and quietly read notes, addresses, and annotations. As we continued, my intimacy with Semyon became more complete.

Finally, there were some tattered pages of the criminal code on corrective labor as well.

Excited and deeply moved by our discoveries, and with difficulty following Olga's rapid Russian, I needed time out to process this information, needed to escape from the building, to run headlong away from it, to feel the sunlight on my face and cleanse myself in fresh air. I wanted to rest my eyes on the poplars, to take deep breaths, to lose myself in the gaiety of flowers and the concreteness of real faces.

I arranged for another visit the following afternoon, when I discovered more surprises. Semyon had apparently been commissioned to write a book—*Moskva Voennaya (Moscow at War)*—a history of Lenin's power politics. The slender and worn copy also contained a bibliographical guide. I was impressed with his analysis of War Communism, the ideological and military battles, the Civil War, and Soviet imperialist ambitions. Again, sitting next to each other, Olga and I read and leafed through more pages.

Only because of her concentrated and professional search were we able to resurrect Semyon Geller from the newspaper *Izvestya*: "'The revolution had raised its flag in Moscow,' Bolsheviks declare, to prove 'graphically the link between Russia's revolution and the fate of the whole world.'"

And, trying to discover what drove him to his fate, I paused at Semyon's passages of Communist orthodox rhetoric that sent him to perish.

"Owners are enemies of the future order. War communism will conquer and destroy the institutions of private property. Glory to the nationalization of land! Monuments of the bourgeoisie must crumble with the destruction of private property!"

Sifting through more of the soft, crumbling layers inside the box, we found still more scraps of ephemera, daily events where real dramas became serialized newspaper stories about the Russian heroes fighting for Peace, Land, and Soviet Power. More pages lay there with pencil marks correcting typos, or noting factual errors and real dramas, as well as notes recording memorial services for deceased journalists and academics.

Semyon emerges as an idealistic communist and an intellectual! He believed the Marxist dialectic was the true "organ of historical awakening" in which one could detect history at its secret work. "With the destabilizing of the market economy, we begin to recognize the monuments of the bourgeoisie as ruins even before they must crumble," he wrote.

His small book read to me like an author's philosophy, explaining his compulsive desire and stubborn intuition that the past might yield its secrets for the future. His fighting spirit lived in that volume and in the scraps of newspaper that supplied a life record of historical events and set the stage for his own tragic fate.

I understood deeply that this country was not exclusively a nosegay of my nanny's fairy tales, or an artefact of my father's native language and the culture he loved. Other aspects of Russia can be uncovered by comparing the old Moscow of the 1970s and '80s to the Moscow that exists today.

In Stalin's time, the city had declared itself a singular feat of urban engineering and the epicenter of the new communist world. Moscow always seethes and bubbles and gasps for air. It's always thirsting for something new—the newest events, the latest sensation. The city of nine million souls wishes to be sophisticated but at times behaves like a village. Everyone wants to be the first to know the latest cultural and political gossip. When I showed up in the late '70s, the city's urban landscape was made up predominantly of its courtyards, streets, and parks—places, that is, where urban inhabitants actually lived and spent their time. Residents referred to the city as a big-village *topos*: an intimate space that continues functioning as a place in which the locals quite simply lead ordinary lives.

After the devastation of World War II, Stalin ordered that

new attention be paid to the capitol, that it be clothed in new symbols of victory and a new era of Soviet ideology and power. Between 1947 and 1957, he erected seven Gothic *vysotky*—towering skyscrapers built by German World War II prisoners. I rented an apartment in one of them, in a residential building for privileged artists adjoining the Hotel Ukraina, facing Kotuzovsky Prospekt—a thoroughfare comparable to upper Madison Avenue in New York.

The city's rhythm of life breathes fire like a human volcano. Back then, the only safe, permissible feelings were those about love and romance. All else was a smoldering lava of careerism, ambition, and politics in a hurly-burly of meetings. Tourists of the world from everywhere came to explore. The sky was the very blue that the cupolas of St. Basil's had been painted for. Its pinks, greens, and golds shimmered as if the only purpose of religion was to cheer political and divine power.

Five years ago, on my last visit, there was wi-fi on the metro, and there were startups in the suburbs, glass towers in the business parks, and rollerbladers on the embankment, walkways, and public conveyances. The facelift continues, and many things are terrible. The first thing you notice is the traffic. In 1990, there were less than a million cars on Moscow's roads. Now there are at least four times that number, and it sometimes feels as if all of them are stuck on the road in front of you.

Shopping is a very different experience as well. "Kiosk capitalism" is gone. Instead, Moscow offers a retail experience every capitalist metropolis will recognize. Supermarkets and malls, nail parlors and jewelers, banks and car showrooms, are everywhere. And oh—there are lots of dentists, for some reason.

My expatriate status shielded me from the grit of the land and created a distance between myself and the people whose monthly salary would not have covered an evening of drinks at the hotel bar. Fluency in Russian, academic studies, and curiosity demanded that I get my fingernails dirty. Academic studies, and the old emotional need to please my father, had encouraged life-long denials. I had to get out of Moscow, listen to interesting people beyond the crazy beehive, and learn about their *byt*, the daily lives of people who did not want to leave, or couldn't.

I needed time—walks in the countryside or in private *da-*

chas to seriously interact with Moscow friends and understand their true-to-life candor.

The real Russian present revealed itself in glimpses, as if through the narrow lens of an antique slide projector, with faded images waiting for light. I discovered and observed personal secrets as if by magic summoned out of the surrounding dark.

When not stuck in long lunches entertaining business counterparts—*bolshiye shishki* (Russian for "big shots"), I often disappeared in the afternoon to investigate interesting folk art and buy Russian antiques in consignment shops (a friend with a diplomatic passport helped with shipments), but I was forced, alas, to return for the Wall Street morning telephone call I dreaded, when I would make Wall Street happy by transmitting positive information and PR—all bullshit.

One day, one of my Russian friends, Valya, a former docent at the Tretyakov Gallery, invited me to see the new exhibit *Russia, the Land and the People*—nostalgia for the good old times when Stalin was a cult and religion.

Entering the exhibit, I came upon a signed sketch of the statue of Lenin. In the 1930s, Stalin's architects began construction of a utopian capital of urban grandiosity. The original project he ordered in 1935 was to create a statue of Lenin standing so high it would extend above the clouds, making a declaration that the secular heaven of Communism on Earth would replace any religious heaven. Directing all eyes upward, Lenin would serve as a looming reminder of the penetrating gaze to which all were now subject.

We viewed many paintings about enthusiastic Stakhanovites (devoted volunteer workers in factories and farms), people who gave birth to Russian Communism, and many of Stalin with adoring and happy faces and smiling eyes of children presenting flowers to the *vozhd* (leader). We contemplated several contemporary bronze reproductions of Lenin's iconic statue in Red Square, with one arm upraised. The pose had been copied in thousands of monuments all over the Soviet Empire, and promised the *narod* (citizen folk) that their grandchildren would be unable to imagine that public buildings on the street had once been someone's property.

Over coffee in Café Chaus (a trendy Moscow coffee house), we discussed the communist interpretation of Lenin's and Stalin's resurrections as new messiahs. Valya was uncomfortable and ill at ease, but finally suggested that we visit her very old grandmother Maria, a historic figure living in a distant village near Stupino, eighty kilometers from Moscow. I was fascinated and intrigued by Valya's story and couldn't wait to speak with this elderly idealistic communist. Maria had personally known and worked closely with Lenin! I imagined that speaking with her would be like picturing a statue of Lenin, his eyes stirring, ready to reveal intimate secrets of his life's work.

We travelled by train. I watched the landscape rolling past the windows and listened to a Russian couple's discussion of how to transport a newly purchased washing machine, and soon drifted off to the clacking of the wheels.

Arriving in Stupino—we had finished our lunch of boiled eggs, cucumbers, and radish salad on the train—we looked for a taxi. An old Volga showed up to show us around the area and drive us to Maria's place. Price: two American dollars! The elderly driver was grateful, chain-smoking Russian Belomorkanal cigarettes, originally sold only to officers. I was sick, nauseated by the strong, foul stench, and fished out a pack of legal tender: Marlboros for him.

Maria was an early, idealistic Communist who worked with Lenin in Germany. Her dream was to rid the world of rulers who sent young men to their deaths, starved their people, and robbed the weak. She believed in worldwide brotherhood and universal shared happiness. Her brother had been killed in the First World War. She spoke several languages, was an activist and wrote propaganda pamphlets for Socialist strikes and rallies. She also assisted Lenin as a courier for a number of secret missions in Switzerland and Berlin. She returned to Russia with him, by train to the Finland Station, and managed Lenin's staff.

In the time of Stalin's great terror, she was arrested as a cosmopolitan and an "enemy of the people." Her husband and family disowned and denounced her to save themselves. Her two children bought their own apartments in Moscow, and have responsible and lucrative jobs. They are embarrassed by their mother.

Others describe her as an old mad woman. When she was finally released from prison, she was poor and had nothing to live on. Many years before, she had been dumped in this lonely village, in an isolated facility which had ironically been designed by one of her engineer sons in charge of construction.

Valya organized a Sunday visit for us. We arrived before noon on a glorious summer day, but the air smelled of rain. Foxtails bobbed above the grass; the meadow, crowded with unending flowers so rich in hues and tints, was like a multicolored carpet or a kaleidoscope.

Further beyond and quite suddenly, the landscape changed—we passed a vast industrial zone of concrete structures and steel cylinders, a tangle of steel pipes and a hissing system to feed it, and a warehouse in ruins.

At last, we reached the village: six or seven *izbas* (huts), the remnants of an orchard, and an abandoned barn that spoke of agricultural activity long ago. The street was lined with collapsing wooden houses, caved-in roofs, molding walls, and missing glass and door hinges.

Beyond the village was the edge of a wood that expanded to a broad valley covered in meadow land, which had not been threatened with scything for a long time. A combine harvester, brown with rust, all its tires flat, lay idle, surrounded by a profusion of grasses and flowers. The sky had become grayer, and wind swept through the trees. Just beyond the wreck of the combine harvester, the meadow sloped more steeply. From above, beyond the thickets, banks of a stream were just visible, a footpath down to it swamped with wild plants. All of it exuded an air of life on the verge of extinction, emptiness, and regret.

Finally, we came to Maria's residence. The walls of the wretched old-age home were painted a very pale blue, like cornflowers on the brink of fading. Inside stretched a long, dark corridor with small windows running along one side and doors on the other. The place resembled a barracks for single women.

We entered the building, slipping along the wall like thieves, while Valya searched for her room. Finally, we met Maria.

Inside the room there was a narrow work table, or rather a desk, where a few books, a pen, and a stack of paper were arranged in perfect order. A volume of Lenin's work lay open on the desk with pencil marks on the page. And there were a sepia photograph showing Lenin and Maria, a simple antiquated lamp, and another old portrait: of a young man dressed in the uniform of a cavalryman in the Red Army, probably the husband who had denounced her.

The small room was filled with two other stacks of books, and the remainder of the walls with snapshots of a color verging on ochre, static portraits that gave away just how old they were. It seemed as if I was looking at a display cabinet in a museum, showing a reconstructed tableau of life in the remote past.

Maria stood tall, proud, and engaging. Her smile was wise and dignified, her head held high like a patriotic Soviet woman, her voice cheerful.

"Welcome!" she said in a strong, well-modulated voice. "Happiness comes unexpectedly. So many thanks for coming to see me. You must be tired—please sit, please."

"Thank you," said Valya. "And here is a friend of mine, Susanna. She's from America."

"All this way," Maria murmured, as she and I nodded at each other, her eyes, I could sense, evaluating me. We sat on plain wooden chairs with hand-made cushions.

"May I offer you some tea?" she asked, and I was about to politely decline when Valya said that would be most appreciated.

The old woman vanished down the narrow hallway and

returned some time later with tea brewing in an old electric pot, unmatched cups and saucers, and a small bowl of sugar on a wooden tray. She poured, and we sipped. "This seems very serviceable," I ventured, after thanking her for the tea, which had instantly revived me.

She looked around. "Yes, in the end it is. A hole in a tree," she added with an unexpected chuckle. "I don't miss my Moscow apartment, you know. But I miss the city. I miss Moscow's *Den' Pobedy*." This was the Day of Victory parade. "I marched twice with Heroes of the Soviet Union, after the Patriotic War. . . . You must remember my dear comrade, Viktoria Sergeevna," she said to Valya. "Not long ago she brought me a tin-metal box of *sushki* and *kartoshki*." They were pretzels and potato-shaped cookies. "Now, she is gone as well. I am happy to be alive—happy in my little world. Now, my old life has fallen into place," she said, sweeping her hand over the room. "When you are old and poor, you don't need a palace, especially when no one loves you."

I had another escape from the city to the countryside with two Moscow friends: Vadim, a geologist, and Sasha, a mathematician. After a pretty complicated and self-conscious intellectual conversation about Communism and Cubism, and another discussing determinism and the scientific method, they suggested we visit an apple orchard. Both had been to that gigantic orchard on a high school trip and were eager to show me the Soviet scientific experiment: a Potemkin village. The mastery of the natural world by Soviet industry and agriculture, a Soviet mentality for constructing the world's largest—locomotive, bulldozer, sugar factory, iron smelter. . . . "All these ideas had one thing in common: senselessness," wrote a Moscow journalist.

The early summer day was magnificent. We travelled by *elektrichka,* an electric tram, stopping in a village where cows still mooed and hens clucked inside the village hut, and the grass and the birch forest had the same sweet smell. There was a feeling of space there, of fields and sky. Trekking forward, we passed what looked like a small private farm that offered up the greenery of rye, a scrap of land with barley, the space behind covered with oats. After that came beds of potatoes, a few immature sunflowers with drooping heads, and a deep-green patch of hemp adjoining a small vista of meadow glistening with color, strewn with bright-red crimson specks of poppies, blue corn-flowers, small golden buttercups, and taller goldenrods.

We passed an old church in *remont* (reconstruction), splendid in dense greenery. Thick, very old trees surrounded its enclosure. After resting, we continued trekking the path to the orchard. Birds were pouring out songs and insects buzzing; pine needles warmed by the sun saturated the air with the thick fragrance of resin. The glades and edges of the forest were covered with delicate pale-blue, pink, and yellow flowers, which caressed more than the sense of sight. And there was the power and enchantment as well that only birds of passage knew where it ended.

Reaching the orchard, Sasha continued, "This place is the whole madness of the Communist system in microcosm. A monstrous orchard with a particular ideological purpose; to create the biggest plantation in the world. A triumph of collectivist agriculture! So when the old crocodiles in the Kremlin drive past from Moscow to here, they can see from their limousines a continuous spread of white. Trees are planted close together unnaturally, according to the Communist plans. This orchard is completely unproductive. No bees want to fly the distance to reach the center. As a result, the flowers are not pollinated and the trees don't bear fruit!" The apple orchard bore foaming blossoms on the boughs, the whipped cream of petals, a white wave spilling the length of the avenue of apple trees. Intoxicated by their scents, which had gradually replaced the air, as if finding ourselves on an unknown planet, we were breathing supernatural perfumes. The orchard dazed us with fragrances.

But did so in perfect silence: there was not one insect, no birds, and unchanging light, only gray clouds in a deep blue sky. No apples would ever grow in that ideal place; it was sterile, "Just like the regime we live in!" Vadim shouted.

At home now in New Jersey, I still remember the orchard's white blossoms and my life in Russia. I still see that silent Communist paradise permanently destroying real life.

I picked a bouquet of wild flowers and carefully placed them on the rack of the *elektrichka*. And we drove back to the teeming streets of Moscow and the frustrating challenge—my personal Holy Grail—the global trading in metals and financial products.

One contact leads to another and one conversation to another discovery. No apples are falling off trees, but there is serendipity! Sasha's grandfather, Andrey Kolmogorov, is the fifth most famous Russian mathematician. His biography has been translated into sixty-five languages! He was appointed director of the Mathematical Research Institute at Moscow University and the Mathematical Institute of the U.S.S.R.

Peredelkino is a writers' colony where Sasha's family owns a *dacha*. One hot summer day, I asked Volodya, our driver, to take us there. Volodya was in a rush; he had to attend to private business along the way. As the city released us, he drove faster, and the spaces between buildings widened under bright sun and a mosaic of gunmetal clouds. We left Moscow on a wide but rough highway with two lanes in each direction; it was treacherously pitted with dips and potholes. He drove recklessly, cutting across lanes, passing grimy boulevards, peeling mansions, and huge Brezhnev-era concrete apartment complexes, only to stop in a kiosk market along the way to buy and sell illicit CDs and videos. On the way a village flickered past us with dilapidated wooden houses and old tin roofs, chimneys with plumes of smoke, and whimsical, carved wooden doors and window frames.

We arrived in Peredelkino safe and sound, though, for relaxation in Sasha's family dacha. In the colony's heyday, many of the cottages had offered sweeping views of the field stretching nearly a mile between the birch alley and the fifteenth-century Church of the Transfiguration. Today, the church and convent are no longer visible, blocked by a mansion complex and overshadowed by a recently constructed temple put up by a billionaire in memory of his mother. The village is increasingly filled with construction by a wave of "new Russians," business-class individuals in post-Soviet society. The original settlers lament the transformation of Peredelkino into a complex of the lavish homes of Muscovites.

Peredelkino was a place that signified the difference between the commonplace and the famed in Russia at the time of its peak existence in the mid- to late-1900s. Before Soviet times, it arose as a *dacha* community outside Moscow for scientists, writers, artists and poets. A typical *dacha* is used as a weekend or summer getaway from the hectic urban life, but *dachas* there were more lavish, and provided creative inspiration to their residents.

We travelled the narrow roads to a wonderland in the *podmoskovie* landscape. I was struck by a feeling of space, fields, and wide expanse of open sky, and along both sides of the road stretched the usual forests of golden pines, larch, spruce, and birch.

Beyond were tall trees and filtered sunlight. The road dipped down into a ravine with a stream at the bottom of it, crossed by a wooden bridge. We parked the car and walked through a splendid forest across ravines, clearings and groves. We didn't need much time in the forest and breathing the sweet air to feel cured, strengthened, and reborn, rested from the tensions of Moscow and its bureaucratic indolence. It was quiet. The late afternoon sun lit the grass and the woods with gold. We stayed in the forest to see the sunset: first red, then violet, then at last the deep blue of twilight. It was difficult to continue walking because of the tranquility and the beauty of the surroundings.

On the way to Sascha's relatives' *dacha*, we passed plots of scrubbed land where old *dachas* had been razed to the ground, and then a gated cluster of well-appointed houses belonging to the privileged: many hideous mansions with turrets and a permanent fence eighteen feet high built for the newly rich.

We arrived. Sascha's smiling wife ceremoniously opened the wooden gate and led us down a short winding path to the cottage as we breathed in the scent of honeysuckle entwined in old wooden slats in the rickety veranda. We apologized for being late and, once inside, were invited directly to the small dining room. Their daughter, Liza Mikhailovna, was in the process of setting the table, a traditional custom of welcome and respect. From the kitchen emanated wonderful smells. Liza carefully placed an antique porcelain tureen on the table and meticulously ladled the first course. We savored a hearty, aromatic, thick, and tasty fish soup (ukha), along with a heap of dumplings with a dollop of sour cream slowly sliding down the rims of our bowls. Followed by the main course: zharkoye, roasted duck with cabbage, which was also scrumptious. Many vodka toasts of welcome and success were exchanged throughout the meal. Dessert consisted of a rhubarb pie (pirog), light and delightful as French pastry, and cherry dumplings with sour cream, with cherry brandy and tea with jam.

In between toasts and conversation, her parents and Liza Mikhailovna spoke of the history and culture of old Russia. After many praises for the banquet and a short post—prandial rest, Liza had plans. She had made arrangements to introduce us to next-door neighbors spending the summer in their antique, untouched mid-century *dacha,* a country house. It had been returned to them in the late 1950s because their lawyer nephew had litigated repossession against the State. This fascinating country cottage resembled a museum archive for future exhibits. The living room was cluttered with old furniture, stuffy sofas, many glass bookcases, a piano, a grandfather clock, and—somehow retrieved—original nineteenth-century paintings.

These people, then in their late eighties, were married in pre-revolutionary times. As survivors of Tsarist Russia, they were white Russians who for mysterious reasons had not escaped to France, as their friends had, but had grown old in the country they could no longer love. Their conversation and manners gave them away as belonging to a different era, to another world, and provided them with an extreme sense of remoteness. They continued to live in a culture they had never really left. It was obvious in the way they spoke, interchanging cultured Russian and French, reviving and revisiting old memories, bright glimpses of their shared past.

The gentleman, still handsome, tall and lean, dressed properly in a *pidzhak*, a house jacket, was helping his disabled wife with the care one exercises for a child. He spoke to her as to a sweet child you admire, as a reminder of her youth, while explaining to us, "In all human sorrows, only the love and faith bring Christ's consolation. *Il ne faut jamais rien outrer.*" And I nodded: One *must* never overdo.

"I was just excited, preparing for our guests," she said. "No, I feel much better now. No, it wasn't my heart, I promise. I was just a bit breathless."

Her speech was slow, though, and disconnected. "Remember those stations after the revolution? That was really pushing and shoving. . .we were still disguised as peasants. There was the day the army guards were all around us, and you began to speak in French. I was really afraid."

"Our *beau frère* had many *nepriyatnosti* to repossess our dacha, and all our furniture." He meant "difficult situations." "We live here as long as we can, until the first autumn snow. Then back to Moscow, to our devoted daughter's apartment. She loves us and watches over us. We are blessed and grateful. *Gospodi pomiluy!*" God have mercy indeed, I thought.

And as long as we are on the subject of the Almighty, I am struck by the absence; aside from the glancing mention of one small church under reconstruction, I haven't yet said a word about the Russian Orthodox Church in this final chapter.

It is perhaps indicative of my own skewed view of that pillar of national identity—or of Russian people's skewed, hesitant view of it—that I am not easily able to find a place for it in my ongoing romance with Russia. Yet it's unmistakably, irrevocably, *there*.

I have always loved the religious "karma" of churches and monasteries as much as the personalities of people I met. I had worked in Russia, after all, for a very long time. After losing Peter and endless grieving, the intense spirituality of Russian Orthodox religious services became my refuge and safety net. I lit candles for Peter in all the churches I visited with a super-religious Russian Orthodox friend.

And I am thinking of the Optina Pustyn monastery, the last great refuge of the hermitic tradition that connected Russia with Byzantium and came to be regarded as the spiritual center of the national consciousness. All the greatest writers of the nineteenth century—Gogol, Dostoevsky, and Tolstoy among them—went there in their search for the "Russian soul." The monastery was cut off from the modern world, inaccessible by the railway or by road in the nineteenth century, and pilgrims who approached the holy shrine, by river boat or on foot, or, to be blessed with a "cure" (as at Lourdes) by crawling on their knees, were often overcome by the sensation of traveling back in time.

We followed a pathway for tourists to the monastery. The road was packed with snow. We were following long-haired monks, in black habits, smirking and staring at two women in spike heels, tight jeans, and short coats navigating the slippery road. We passed a *lavka,* a small shop staffed by a young nun that sold fresh bread, purple wine in plastic bottles, mead, and soft *pryaniki,* honey cakes filled with plum jam. On another table, another nun was selling religious items, candles, incense, and small hand-crafted icons.

This monastery was devoted to the contemplative life and the belief that God cannot be grasped by the human mind. Famous as a clinic for spiritual rebirth and divine grace, a mystical experience of humility in passive suffering, the emotional encounter with liturgy as a spiritual entry into the divine realm, the monastery's churches are heavenly gates open on all sides, and dense clouds of smoky incense hang in the air around the candelabra. Wherever you look there are lights, brightness, and candles sputtering. I lit one for Peter. There are no planned readings, but the joyful singing does not stop until the end. You hear a constant repetition of melodies, and the service is very long. I was struck by the minor chords and the yearning timbre of the Slavic voices, which conjured images of emotional closure. Yes, the Church has a deeply blemished record of collusion with secular authority, had in many ways a murky relationship with the Soviet Empire, and seems profoundly compromised in the Age of Putin. But those sputtering candles are real, not metaphorical, and they have offered consolation to the average Russian for centuries.

I escaped to Russia after months of crying and grieving for Peter everywhere, most of all with a Freudian analyst. Before long, Eliot was diagnosed with AIDS, a fatal disease at the time, another Holocaust. I had been betrayed, was desperate, bewildered, an orphan in denial. I tested frequently for AIDS as well; the results were all negative. I had ongoing panic attacks.

In the real AIG world, promoted to vice-president and representative for the new Moscow outpost I was mandated to organize, I had no help, no advice, just plenty of chutzpa, my own resilience, and support from Gary Davis. I flew alone. My job was to find and organize an AIG office for trading and financial services, the newest strategic outpost for the company.

AIG's project in Moscow was fantasy come true, a dream, a clean getaway. Gary Davis and Hank Greenberg waved their magic wands, and I was finally permitted to get away! I wanted to *live!* I abandoned Lisa and Jonathan to struggle with their tragedies and fled to Russia, my father's first language and culture, *and my idea of Russia*—born of its literature, art, music and dance. I was thrilled! I loved the melodic language. I tried, but failed to speak with a Moscow accent. I loved the creativity of artists—whether paintings in museums or folk art in villages. Artists combine European classicism with a native sensibility that liberated Russian culture, a "Russianness," from many European influences. These insights have their own curious logic, and my romance with Russia continued with maestro Valery Gergiev conducting Russian operas at the Metropolitan Opera, Russian ballet, and occasional performances of Russian theater.

Russians generally have a close emotional connection to their history. The recent past has been integral in shaping the nation and the society today. To understand Russian people, one must appreciate that they have survived two revolutions, two world wars, and a civil war in the 20th century, as well as socioeconomic and political upheavals that wrenched their lives both during and after. A systemic socioeconomic breakdown in the 1990s impoverished many and affected people's lifestyles as well as their visions for the future.

A sense of melancholy and nostalgia may become noticeable in conversations when older Russians discuss the past. *Ransche bylo luchshe,* they say: Our earlier lives were better. The Soviet Union is often associated with stability. Older Russians may long for the time when the USSR was a global superpower. Generally, though, the older generation has a more pessimistic and fatalistic perspective, having experienced the time when the Soviet state was responsible for and determined their well-being. Now they have a reduced sense of control over their lives and are resigned to the idea that it is out of their hands.

Now in my eighth decade, my mind's eye is still dazzled by the wide open, endless Russian skies, capricious and frivolous facades of old buildings, the pristine rivers, the open, snow-white horizons of the Siberian steppe, grass and earth, frozen space made into an instrument of political repression.

Not the language, not food, not architecture, not the landscapes, countryside, but certainly the people, remain Russia's greatest treasure. My relationships with Russian friends, their respect for music and literature, sarcastic sense of humor, and anger (helped by vodka around the kitchen table) endure. I remember the celebration of warm spring weather in Moscow—happiness can be an emotional process. Bare-chested men sunbathing, taking in the warm sun—*solntse greet*—and women impeccably dressed, like models promenading arm in arm, window shopping on Tverskaya Street and meticulously analyzing and conversing before the windows of Gucci, Ralph Lauren, Jaeger, Prada, are chiseled in my mind.

I loved, studied and bought antiques and paintings in the consignment shop in the Arbat area. I admired views of the Hotel National and the Bolshoi Theater standing in all its glory at Alexander Gates. As Gary Davis often cynically remarked, "We opened a commercial office in Moscow for shopping and the Bolshoi Ballet."

Moonlight by the Kremlin walls prefigured my disen-chantment—a break in the strong emotional tide to Mother Russia. AIG's financial losses destroyed my personal ambitions. My romance faded. I realized then that loving and understanding Russia would also prevent me from living there.

The crudities of the political system, and its managers, were not the only cause. I always felt an alienating chill in the air. There were too many bureaucratic annoyances, too many expressions of bad manners, and occasional demonstrations of racism as well. There was a lot of petty and no-so-petty stuff. Back in Brezhnev's time, life may not have been entirely sweet, but at least we knew that tomorrow would be like yesterday and today. We could count on *zastoy* (stagnation), comfort, and stability. I once left a mink coat on a hotel lobby armchair while hosting a long restaurant lunch. When I returned hours later, the coat was still in the same place. By comparison, in Putin's time, a motorcyclist grabbed my handbag, hurting my shoulder, and took off. Of course, these are mere anecdotes, but I believe they're telling.

I must confess: Working permanently in Moscow, I was

very self-involved and naively trusted that my charm, good looks, and smarts would be sufficient to finalize the infrastructure for the AIG office and our business. I was solipsistic enough to believe our Soviet counterparts in the platinum group metals bureaucracy were fascinated enough with my background and personality to approve AIG's plans, blinded by the sense that AIG was a multinational giant, and that our strategic project would perforce be successful. It all depended on me--a superwoman slaying Goliath.

I was, in fact, in total denial, my head in the sand. Arriving in America as a teenager, the imperative had been to assimilate into American culture. Being the best and being most competitive seemed to me what America was all about. Success in America confirmed my European extended family's view of me as the best and the brightest. I learned about humility, compassion, and empathy very late in life, only after retirement. Never in business school, I paid scant attention to the government's strategic plans, foreign policy, or Russian paranoia. "Yes," these functionaries must have been thinking, "foreigners bring expensive gifts and organize classy receptions—but they're not really quite human, are they? They only *appear* to be like us, but they don't have *souls*, they're empty. . .we will always trick them, but they cannot trick us. Zolotaya Susanna is an American, a foreigner perhaps also working for the FBI or CIA."

In the last twenty years, big changes in materialism and individualism have emerged in Russia. When I was last in Moscow, the primary aspiration of Russians across all demographics was to secure stable jobs and futures to see their children be more prosperous and successful. Cultural shifts towards individualism have always been easier for the educated and urbanized. Putin's acolytes are enjoying newfound success in a growing middle class at home and as the super-rich in Western countries or Dubai enjoying their yachts and villas. Those raised in the post-socialist period often have different attitudes from Russians who lived through the Soviet era. The generational divide is commonly more optimistic as urbanites find ways to successfully maneuver around sanctions. They often are more hopeful regarding the future as well, have more fun, and are flexible and open with sarcasm, humor and anger.

The last time I was in Moscow, having lunch at the famous

McDonald's (no longer in business), a young man, probably a university student, broke the long queue, pushed his way in, and threw a dead un-plucked chicken at the cashier, shouting loudly with colorful swear words about the recent quality of chicken tenders. The customers remained silent but shocked as he quietly walked out without being stopped or arrested. Today, such an incident would result in jail time.

Russian history revealed itself intimately in Russians I befriended, eager to expose me to the real lifestyle of these fascinating personalities. It has taken me a long time to understand Russia, almost as long as myself.

This last chapter has been the most difficult to write. Having studied and analyzed the politics and culture of the country my whole life, my experiences and views of Russia have been hard to condense—but I must end. Since endings are arbitrary, here is mine: if I were a lot younger, I would be back in Moscow, sitting around a kitchen table with my Russian friends. Or to quote Friedrich Nietzsche, "Evil men have no songs. How is it that the Russians have songs?"

This book has been set in Hoefler's *Requiem*, derived from a set of inscriptional capitals appearing in Ludovico Vicentino degli Arrighi's 1523 writing manual, *Il Modo de Temparere le Penne*.